The Fatal Dowry by Philip Massinger & Nathaniel Field

A TRAGEDY - As it hath beene often Acted at the Priuate House in Blackefryers, by his Maiesties Seruants.

Philip Massinger was baptized at St. Thomas's in Salisbury on November 24th, 1583.

Massinger is described in his matriculation entry at St. Alban Hall, Oxford (1602), as the son of a gentleman. His father, who had also been educated there, was a member of parliament, and attached to the household of Henry Herbert, 2nd Earl of Pembroke. The Earl was later seen as a potential patron for Massinger.

He left Oxford in 1606 without a degree. His father had died in 1603, and accounts suggest that Massinger was left with no financial support this, together with rumours that he had converted to Catholicism, meant the next stage of his career needed to provide an income.

Massinger went to London to make his living as a dramatist, but he is only recorded as author some fifteen years later, when The Virgin Martyr (1621) is given as the work of Massinger and Thomas Dekker.

During those early years as a playwright he wrote for the Elizabethan stage entrepreneur, Philip Henslowe. It was a difficult existence. Poverty was always close and there was constant pleading for advance payments on forthcoming works merely to survive.

After Henslowe died in 1616 Massinger and John Fletcher began to write primarily for the King's Men and Massinger would write regularly for them until his death.

The tone of the dedications in later plays suggests evidence of his continued poverty. In the preface of The Maid of Honour (1632) he wrote, addressing Sir Francis Foljambe and Sir Thomas Bland: "I had not to this time subsisted, but that I was supported by your frequent courtesies and favours."

The prologue to The Guardian (1633) refers to two unsuccessful plays and two years of silence, when the author feared he had lost popular favour although, from the little evidence that survives, it also seems he had involved some of his plays with political characters which would have cast shadows upon England's alliances.

Philip Massinger died suddenly at his house near the Globe Theatre on March 17th, 1640. He was buried the next day in the churchyard of St. Saviour's, Southwark, on March 18th, 1640. In the entry in the parish register he is described as a "stranger," which, however, implies nothing more than that he belonged to another parish.

Index of Contents

INTRODUCTION
DATE
Dramatis Personae
ACT PRIMUS

SCENE I - A Street Before the Court of Justice
SCENE II - The Court of Justice
ACT SECONDUS
SCENE I - A Street Before the Prison
SCENE II - A Room in Rochfort's House.
ACTUS TERTIUS
SCENE I - A Room in Charalois' House
ACTUS QUARTUS
SCENE I - A Room in Nouall's House
SCENE II - An Outer Room in Aymer's House
SCENE III - A Street
SCENE IV - A Room in Charalois' House
ACTUS QUINTUS
SCENE I - A Street
SCENE II - The Court of Justice
SCENE III
SOURCES
COLLABORATION
STAGE HISTORY—ADAPTATIONS—DERIVATIVES
PHILIP MASSINGER – A SHORT BIOGRAPHY
PHILIP MASSINGER – A CONCISE BIBLIOGRAPHY

INTRODUCTION

In the Stationer's Register the following entry is recorded under the date of "30º Martij 1632:"

CONSTABLE Entred for his copy vnder the hands of Sir HENRY HERBERT and master SMITHWICKE warden a Tragedy called the ffatall Dowry.

In the year 1632 was published a quarto volume whose title-page was inscribed: The Fatall Dowry: a Tragedy: As it hath been often Acted at the Private House in Blackfriars, by his Majesties Servants. Written by P. M. and N. F. London, Printed by John Norton, for Francis Constable, and are to be sold at his shop at the Crane, in Pauls Churchyard. 1632.

That the initials by which the authors are designated stand for Philip Massinger and Nathaniel Field is undoubted.

DATE

The date of the composition or original production of The Fatal Dowry is not known. The Quarto speaks of it as having been "often acted," so there is nothing to prevent our supposing that it came into existence many years before its publication. It does not seem to have been entered in Sir Henry Herbert's Office Book. This would indicate its appearance to have been prior to Herbert's assumption of the duties of his office in August, 1623. In seeking a more precise date we can deal only in probabilities.

The play having been produced by the King's Men, a company in which Field acted, it was most probably written during his association therewith. This was formed in 1616; the precise date of his retirement from the stage is not known. His name appears in the patent of March 27, 1619, just after the death of Burbage, and again and for the last time in a livery list for his Majesty's Servants, dated May 19, 1619. It is absent from the next grant for livery (1621) and from the actors' lists for various plays which are assigned to 1619 or 1620. We may therefore assume safely that his connection with the stage ended before the close of 1619. On the basis of probability, then, the field is narrowed to 1616-19.

More or less presumptive evidence may be adduced for a yet more specific dating. During these years that Field acted with the King's Men, two plays appeared which bear strong internal evidence of being products of his collaboration with Massinger and Fletcher: The Knight of Malta and The Queen of Corinth. While several parallels of phraseology are afforded for The Fatal Dowry by these (as, indeed, by every one of the works of Massinger) they are not nearly so numerous or so striking as similarities discoverable between it and certain other dramas of the Massinger corpus. With none does the connection seem so intimate as with The Unnatural Combat. Both plays open with a scene in which a young suppliant for a father's cause is counseled, in passages irresistibly reminiscent of each other, to lay aside pride and modesty for the parent's sake, because not otherwise can justice be gained, and it is the custom of the age to sue for it shamelessly. Moreover, the offer by Beaufort and his associates to Malefort of any boon he may desire as a recompense for his service, and his acceptance of it, correspond strikingly in both conduct and language with the conferring of a like favor upon Rochfort by the Court (I, ii, 258 ff.); while the request which Malefort prefers, that his daughter be married to Beaufort Junior, and the language with which that young man acknowledges this meets his own dearest wish, bear a no less patent resemblance to the bestowal of Beaumelle upon Charalois (II, ii, 284-297). Now this last parallel is significant, because The Unnatural Combat is an unaided production of Massinger, while the analogue in The Fatal Dowry occurs in a scene that is by the hand of Field. The similarity may, of course, be only an accident, but presumably it is not. Then did Field borrow from Massinger, or did Massinger from Field? The most plausible theory is that The Unnatural Combat was written immediately after The Fatal Dowry, when Massinger's mind was so saturated with the contents of the tragedy just laid aside that he was liable to echo in the new drama the expressions and import of lines in the old, whether by himself or his collaborator. That at any rate the chronological relationship of the two plays is one of juxtaposition is further attested by the fact that in minor parallelisms, too, to The Fatal Dowry, The Unnatural Combat is richer than any other work of Massinger.

Unfortunately The Unnatural Combat is itself another play of whose date no more can be said with assurance than that it precedes the entry of Sir Henry Herbert into office in 1623, though its crude horrors, its ghost, etc., suggest moreover that it is its author's initial independent venture in the field of tragedy, his Titus Andronicus, an ill-advised attempt to produce something after the "grand manner" of half a generation back. Next in closeness to The Fatal Dowry among the works of Massinger as regards the number of its reminiscences of phraseology stands his share of The Virgin Martyr; next in closeness as regards the strikingness of these parallels stands his share of The Little French Lawyer. These two plays can be dated circa 1620.

Dramatis Personae

Charalois.
Romont.

Charmi
Nouall Senior
Liladam.
DuCroy.
Rochfort.
Baumont.
Pontalier.
Malotin.
Beaumelle.
Florimel.
Bellapert.
Aymer.
Nouall Junior
Aduocates.
Creditors 3.
Officers.
Priest.
Taylor.
Barber.
Perfumer.

Presidents, Captains, Soldiers, Mourners, Gaoler, Bailiffs, Servants.

ACT PRIMUS

SCENE I

A Street Before the Court of Justice

Enter **CHARALOIS** with a paper, **ROMONT**, **CHARMI**.

CHARMI
Sir, I may moue the Court to serue your will,
But therein shall both wrong you and my selfe.

ROMONT
Why thinke you so sir?

CHARMI
'Cause I am familiar
With what will be their answere: they will say,
'Tis against law, and argue me of Ignorance
For offering them the motion.

ROMONT
You know not, Sir,
How in this cause they may dispence with Law,
And therefore frame not you their answere for them,
But doe your parts.

CHARMI
I loue the cause so well,
As I could runne, the hazard of a checke for ’t.

ROMONT
From whom?

CHARMI
Some of the bench, that watch to give it,
More then to doe the office that they fit for:
But giue me (sir) my fee.

ROMONT
Now you are Noble.

CHARMI
I shall deserue this better yet, in giuing
My Lord some counsell, (if he please to heare it)
Then I shall doe with pleading.

ROMONT
What may it be, sir?

CHARMI
That it would please his Lordship, as the presidents,
And Counsaylors of Court come by, to stand
Heere, and but shew your selfe, and to some one
Or two, make his request: there is a minute
When a mans presence speakes in his owne cause,
More then the tongues of twenty aduocates.

ROMONT
I haue vrg’d that.

[Enter **ROCHFORT**, **Du CROY**.

CHARMI
Their Lordships here are coming,
I must goe get me a place, you’l finde me in Court,
And at your seruice

[Exit **CHARMI**.

ROMONT
Now put on your Spirits.

Du CROY
The ease that you prepare your selfe, my Lord,
In giuing vp the place you hold in Court,
Will proue (I feare) a trouble in the State,
And that no slight one.

ROCHFORT
Pray you sir, no more.

ROMONT
Now sir, lose not this offerd means: their lookes
Fixt on you, with a pittying earnestnesse,
Inuite you to demand their furtherance
To your good purpose.—This such a dulnesse
So foolish and vntimely as—

Du CROY
You know him.

ROCHFORT
I doe, and much lament the sudden fall
Of his braue house. It is young Charloyes.
Sonne to the Marshall, from whom he inherits
His fame and vertues onely.

ROMONT
Ha, they name you.

Du CROY
His father died in prison two daies since.

ROCHFORT
Yes, to the shame of this vngrateful State;
That such a Master in the art of warre,
So noble, and so highly meriting,
From this forgetfull Country, should, for want
Of meanes to satisfie his creditors,
The summes he tooke vp for the generall good,
Meet with an end so infamous.

ROMONT
Dare you euer
Hope for like opportunity?

Du CROY
My good Lord!

ROCHFORT
My wish bring comfort to you.

Du CROY
The time calls vs.

ROCHFORT
Good morrow Colonell.

[Exeunt **ROCHFORT. Du CROY**.

ROMONT
This obstinate spleene,
You thinke becomes your sorrow, and sorts wel
With your blacke suits: but grant me wit, or iudgement,
And by the freedome of an honest man,
And a true friend to boote, I sweare 'tis shamefull.
And therefore flatter not your selfe with hope,
Your sable habit, with the hat and cloake,
No though the ribons helpe, haue power to worke 'em
To what you would: for those that had no eyes,
To see the great acts of your father, will not,
From any fashion sorrow can put on,
Bee taught to know their duties.

CHARALOIS
If they will not,
They are too old to learne, and I too young
To giue them counsell, since if they partake
The vnderstanding, and the hearts of men,
They will preuent my words and teares: if not,
What can perswasion, though made eloquent
With griefe, worke vpon such as haue chang'd natures
With the most sauage beast? Blest, blest be euer
The memory of that happy age, when iustice
Had no gards to keepe off wrongd innocence,
From flying to her succours, and in that
Assurance of redresse: where now Romont
The damnd, with more ease may ascend from Hell,
Then we ariue at her. One Cerberus there
Forbids the passage, in our Courts a thousand,
As lowd, and fertyle headed, and the Client
That wants the sops, to fill their rauenous throats,
Must hope for no accesse: why should I then
Attempt impossibilities: you friend, being

Too well acquainted with my dearth of meanes,
To make my entrance that way?

ROMONT
Would I were not.
But Sir, you haue a cause, a cause so iust,
Of such necessitie, not to be deferd,
As would compell a mayde, whose foot was neuer
Set ore her fathers threshold, nor within
The house where she was borne, euer spake word,
Which was not vshered with pure virgin blushes,
To drowne the tempest of a pleaders tongue,
And force corruption to giue backe the hire
It tooke against her: let examples moue you.
You see great men in birth, esteeme and fortune,
Rather then lose a scruple of their right,
Fawne basely vpon such, whose gownes put off,
They would disdaine for Seruants.

CHARALOIS
And to these
Can I become a suytor?

ROMONT
Without losse,
Would you consider, that to game their fauors,
Our chastest dames put off their modesties,
Soldiers forget their honors, vsurers
Make sacrifice of Gold, poets of wit,
And men religious, part with fame, and goodnesse?
Be therefore wonne to vse the meanes, that may
Aduance your pious ends.

CHARALOIS
You shall orecome.

ROMONT
And you receiue the glory, pray you now practise.
'Tis well.

[Enter **NOUALL SENIOR, LILLADAM** & **3 CREDITORS**.

CHARALOIS
Not looke on me!

ROMONT
You must haue patience—
Offer't againe.

CHARALOIS
And be againe contemn'd?

NOUALL SENIOR
I know whats to be done.

1ST CREDITOR
And that your Lordship
Will please to do your knowledge, we offer, first
Our thankefull hearts heere, as a bounteous earnest
To what we will adde.

NOUALL SENIOR
One word more of this
I am your enemie. Am I a man
Your bribes can worke on? ha?

LILLADAM
Friends, you mistake
The way to winne my Lord, he must not heare this,
But I, as one in fauour, in his sight,
May harken to you for my profit. Sir,
I pray heare em.

NOUALL SENIOR
Tis well.

LILLADAM
Obserue him now.

NOUALL SENIOR
Your cause being good, and your proceedings so,
Without corruption; I am your friend,
Speake your desires.

2ND CREDITOR
Oh, they are charitable,
The Marshall stood ingag'd vnto vs three,
Two hundred thousand crownes, which by his death
We are defeated of. For which great losse
We ayme at nothing but his rotten flesh,
Nor is that cruelty.

1ST CREDITOR
I haue a sonne,
That talkes of nothing but of Gunnes and Armors,
And sweares hee'll be a soldier, tis an humor

I would diuert him from, and I am told
That if I minister to him in his drinke
Powder, made of this banquerout Marshalls bones,
Provided that the carcase rot aboue ground
'Twill cure his foolish frensie.

NOUALL SENIOR
You shew in it
A fathers care. I haue a sonne my selfe,
A fashionable Gentleman and a peacefull:
And but I am assur'd he's not so giuen,
He should take of it too, Sir what are you?

CHARALOIS
A Gentleman.

NOUALL SENIOR
So are many that rake dunghills.
If you haue any suit, moue it in Court.
I take no papers in corners.

ROMONT
Yes
As the matter may be carried, and hereby
To mannage the conuayance—Follow him.

LILLADAM
You are rude. I say, he shall not passe.

[Exit **NOUALL SENIOR, CHARALOIS** and **ADUOCATES**.

ROMONT
You say so.
On what assurance?
For the well cutting of his Lordships cornes,
Picking his toes, or any office else
Neerer to basenesse!

LILLADAM
Looke vpon mee better,
Are these the ensignes of so coorse a fellow?
Be well aduis'd.

ROMONT
Out, rogue, do not I know,

[Kicks him]

These glorious weedes spring from the sordid dunghill
Of thy officious basenesse? wert thou worthy
Of anything from me, but my contempt,
I would do more then this, more, you Court-spider.

LILLADAM
But that this man is lawlesse;
he should find that I am valiant.

1ST CREDITOR
If your eares are fast,
Tis nothing. Whats a blow or two? As much—

2ND CREDITOR
These chastisements, as vsefull are as frequent
To such as would grow rich.

ROMONT
Are they so Rascals?
I will be-friend you then.

1ST CREDITOR
Beare witnesse, Sirs.

LILLADAM
Trueth, I haue borne my part already, friends.
In the Court you shall haue more.

[Exit.

ROMONT
I know you for
The worst of spirits, that striue to rob the tombes
Of what is their inheritance, from the dead.
For vsurers, bred by a riotous peace:
That hold the Charter of your wealth & freedome,
By being Knaues and Cuckolds that ne're prayd,
But when you feare the rich heires will grow wise,
To keepe their Lands out of your parchment toyles:
And then, the Diuell your father's cald vpon,
To inuent some ways of Luxury ne're thought on.
Be gone, and quickly, or Ile leaue no roome
Vpon your forhead for your hornes to sprowt on,
Without a murmure, or I will vndoe you;
For I will beate you honest.

1ST CREDITOR
Thrift forbid.

We will beare this, rather then hazard that.

[Exit **CREDITOR**.

[Enter **CHARALOIS**.

ROMONT
I am some-what eas'd in this yet.

CHARALOIS
Onely friend
To what vaine purpose do I make my sorrow,
Wayte on the triumph of their cruelty?
Or teach their pride from my humilitie,
To thinke it has orecome? They are determin'd
What they will do: and it may well become me,
To robbe them of the glory they expect
From my submisse intreaties.

ROMONT
Thinke not so, Sir,
The difficulties that you incounter with,
Will crowne the vndertaking—Heaven! you weepe:
And I could do so too, but that I know,
Theres more expected from the sonne and friend
Of him, whose fatall losse now shakes our natures,
Then sighs, or teares, (in which a village nurse
Or cunning strumpet, when her knaue is hangd,
May ouercome vs.) We are men (young Lord)
Let vs not do like women. To the Court,
And there speake like your birth: wake sleeping justice,
Or dare the Axe. This is a way will sort
With what you are. I call you not to that
I will shrinke from my selfe, I will deserue
Your thankes, or suffer with you—O how bravely
That sudden fire of anger shewes in you!
Give fuell to it, since you are on a shelfe,
Of extreme danger suffer like your selfe.

[Exeunt.

SCENE II

The Court of Justice

Enter **ROCHFORT**, **NOUALL SENIOR, CHARMI, Du CROY, ADUOCATES, BAUMONT**, and **OFFICERS**, and **3 PRESIDENTS**.

Du CROY
Your Lordship's seated. May this meeting proue prosperous
to vs, and to the generall good
Of Burgundy.

NOUALL SENIOR
Speake to the poynt.

Du CROY
Which is,
With honour to dispose the place and power
Of primier President, which this reuerent man
Graue Rochfort, (whom for honours sake I name)
Is purpos'd to resigne a place, my Lords,
In which he hath with such integrity,
Perform'd the first and best parts of a Iudge,
That as his life transcends all faire examples
Of such as were before him in Dijon,
So it remaines to those that shall succeed him,
A President they may imitate, but not equall.

ROCHFORT
I may not sit to heare this.

Du CROY
Let the loue
And thankfulnes we are bound to pay to goodnesse,
In this o'recome your modestie.

ROCHFORT
My thankes
For this great fauour shall preuent your trouble.
The honourable trust that was impos'd
Vpon my weaknesse since you witnesse for me,
It was not ill discharg'd, I will not mention,
Nor now, if age had not depriu'd me of
The little strength I had to gouerne well,
The Prouince that I vndertooke, forsake it.

NOUALL SENIOR
That we could lend you of our yeeres.

Du CROY
Or strength.

NOUALL SENIOR
Or as you are, perswade you to continue
The noble exercise of your knowing iudgement.

ROCHFORT
That may not be, nor can your Lordships goodnes,
Since your imployments haue confer'd vpon me
Sufficient wealth, deny the vse of it,
And though old age, when one foot's in the graue,
In many, when all humors else are spent
Feeds no affection in them, but desire
To adde height to the mountaine of their riches:
In me it is not so, I rest content
With the honours, and estate I now possesse,
And that I may haue liberty to vse,
What Heauen still blessing my poore industry,
Hath made me Master of: I pray the Court
To ease me of my burthen, that I may
Employ the small remainder of my life,
In liuing well, and learning how to dye so.

[Enter **ROMONT**, and **CHARALOIS**.

ROMONT
See sir, our Aduocate.

Du CROY
The Court intreats,
Your Lordship will be pleasd to name the man,
Which you would haue your successor, and in me,
All promise to confirme it.

ROCHFORT
I embrace it,
As an assurance of their fauour to me,
And name my Lord Nouall.

Du CROY
The Court allows it.

ROCHFORT
But there are suters waite heere, and their causes
May be of more necessity to be heard,
And therefore wish that mine may be defer'd,
And theirs haue hearing.

Du CROY
If your Lordship please

To take the place, we will proceed.

CHARMI
The cause
We come to offer to your Lordships censure,
Is in it selfe so noble, that it needs not
Or Rhetorique in me that plead, or fauour
From your graue Lordships, to determine of it.
Since to the prayse of your impartiall iustice
(Which guilty, nay condemn'd men, dare not scandall)
It will erect a trophy of your mercy
With married to that Iustice.

NOUALL SENIOR
Speaks to the cause.

CHARMI
I will, my Lord: to say, the late dead Marshall
The father of this young Lord heer, my Clyent,
Hath done his Country great and faithfull seruice,
Might taske me of impertinence to repeate,
What your graue Lordships cannot but remember,
He in his life, become indebted to
These thriftie men, I will not wrong their credits,
By giuing them the attributes they now merit,
And fayling by the fortune of the warres,
Of meanes to free himselfe, from his ingagements,
He was arrested, and for want of bayle
Imprisond at their suite: and not long after
With losse of liberty ended his life.
And though it be a Maxime in our Lawes,
All suites dye with the person, these mens malice
In death find matter for their hate to worke on,
Denying him the decent Rytes of buriall,
Which the sworne enemies of the Christian faith
Grant freely to their slaues, may it therefore please
Your Lordships, so to fashion your decree,
That what their crueltie doth forbid, your pittie
May giue allowance to.

NOUALL SENIOR
How long haue you Sir
Practis'd in Court?

CHARMI
Some twenty yeeres, my Lord.

NOUALL SENIOR

By your grosse ignorance it should appeare,
Not twentie dayes.

CHARMI
I hope I haue giuen no cause
In this, my Lord—

NOUALL SENIOR
How dare you moue the Court,
To the dispensing with an Act confirmd
By Parlament, to the terror of all banquerouts?
Go home, and with more care peruse the Statutes:
Or the next motion fauoring of this boldnesse,
May force you to leape (against your will)
Ouer the place you plead at.

CHARMI
I foresaw this.

ROMONT
Why does your Lordship thinke, the mouing of
A cause more honest then this Court had euer
The honor to determine, can deserue
A checke like this?

NOUALL SENIOR
Strange boldnes!

ROMONT
Tis fit freedome:
Or do you conclude, an aduocate cannot hold
His credit with the Iudge, vnlesse he study
His face more then the cause for which he pleades?

CHARMI
Forbeare.

ROMONT
Or cannot you, that haue the power
To qualifie the rigour of the Lawes,
When you are pleased, take a little from
The strictnesse of your fowre decrees, enacted
In fauor of the greedy creditors
Against the orethrowne debter?

NOUALL SENIOR
Sirra, you that prate
Thus sawcily, what are you?

ROMONT
Why Ile tell you,
Thou purple-colour'd man, I am one to whom
Thou owest the meanes thou hast of sitting there
A corrupt Elder.

CHARMI
Forbeare.

ROMONT
The nose thou wearst, is my gift, and those eyes
That meete no obiect so base as their Master,
Had bin, long since, torne from that guiltie head,
And thou thy selfe slaue to some needy Swisse,
Had I not worne a sword, and vs'd it better
Then in thy prayers thou ere didst thy tongue.

NOUALL SENIOR
Shall such an Insolence passe vnpunisht?

CHARMI
Heere mee.

ROMONT
Yet I, that in my seruice done my Country,
Disdaine to bee put in the scale with thee,
Confesse my selfe vnworthy to bee valued
With the least part, nay haire of the dead Marshall,
Of whose so many glorious vndertakings,
Make choice of any one, and that the meanest
Performd against the subtill Fox of France,
The politique Lewis, or the more desperate Swisse,
And 'twyll outwaygh all the good purpose,
Though put in act, that euer Gowneman practizd.

NOUALL SENIOR
Away with him to prison.

ROMONT
If that curses,
Vrg'd iustly, and breath'd forth so, euer fell
On those that did deserue them; let not mine
Be spent in vaine now, that thou from this instant
Mayest in thy feare that they will fall vpon thee,
Be sensible of the plagues they shall bring with them.
And for denying of a little earth,
To couer what remaynes of our great soldyer:

May all your wiues proue whores, your factors theeues,
And while you liue, your riotous heires vndoe you,
And thou, the patron of their cruelty.
Of all thy Lordships liue not to be owner
Of so much dung as will conceale a Dog,
Or what is worse, thy selfe in. And thy yeeres,
To th' end thou mayst be wretched, I wish many,
And as thou hast denied the dead a graue,
May misery in thy life make thee desire one,
Which men and all the Elements keepe from thee:
I haue begun well, imitate, exceed.

ROCHFORT
Good counsayle were it, a prayse worthy deed.

[Exit **OFFICERS** with **ROMONT**.

Du CROY
Remember what we are.

CHARALOIS
Thus low my duty
Answeres your Lordships counsaile. I will vse
In the few words (with which I am to trouble
Your Lordships eares) the temper that you wish mee.
Not that I feare to speake my thoughts as lowd,
And with a liberty beyond Romont:
But that I know, for me that am made vp
Of all that's wretched, so to haste my end,
Would seeme to most, rather a willingnesse
To quit the burthen of a hopelesse life,
Then scorne of death, or duty to the dead.
I therefore bring the tribute of my prayse
To your seueritie, and commend the Iustice,
That will not for the many seruices
That any man hath done the Common wealth
Winke at his least of ills: what though my father
Writ man before he was so, and confirmd it,
By numbring that day, no part of his life,
In which he did not seruice to his Country;
Was he to be free therefore from the Lawes,
And ceremonious forme in your decrees?
Or else because he did as much as man
In those three memorable ouerthrowes
At Granson, Morat, Nancy, where his Master,
The warlike Charloyes (with whose misfortunes
I beare his name) lost treasure, men and life,
To be excus'd, from payment of those summes

Which (his owne patri mony spent) his zeale,
To serue his Countrey, forc'd him to take vp?

NOUALL SENIOR
The president were ill.

CHARALOIS
And yet, my Lord, this much
I know youll grant; After those great defeatures,
Which in their dreadfull ruines buried quick,

[Enter **OFFICERS**.

Courage and hope, in all men but himselfe,
He forst the proud foe, in his height of conquest,
To yield vnto an honourable peace.
And in it saued an hundred thousand liues,
To end his owne, that was sure proofe against
The scalding Summers heate, and Winters frost,
Illayres, the Cannon, and the enemies sword,
In a most loathsome prison.

Du CROY
Twas his fault
To be so prodigall.

NOUALL SENIOR
He had frô the state
Sufficent entertainment for the Army.

CHARALOIS
Sufficient? My Lord, you sit at home,
And though your fees are boundlesse at the barre:
Are thriftie in the charges of the warre,
But your wills be obeyd. To these I turne,
To these soft-hearted men, that wisely know
They are onely good men, that pay what they owe.

2ND CREDITOR
And so they are.

1ST CREDITOR
'Tis the City Doctrine,
We stand bound to maintaine it.

CHARALOIS
Be constant in it,
And since you are as mercilesse in your natures,

As base, and mercenary in your meanes
By which you get your wealth, I will not vrge
The Court to take away one scruple from
The right of their lawes, or one good thought
In you to mend your disposition with.
I know there is no musique in your eares
So pleasing as the groanes of men in prison,
And that the teares of widows, and the cries
Of famish'd Orphants, are the feasts that take you.
That to be in your danger, with more care
Should be auoyded, then infectious ayre,
The loath'd embraces of diseased women,
A flatterers poyson, or the losse of honour.
Yet rather then my fathers reuerent dust
Shall want a place in that faire monument,
In which our noble Ancestors lye intomb'd,
Before the Court I offer vp my selfe
A prisoner for it: loade me with those yrons
That haue worne out his life, in my best strength
Ile run to th' incounter of cold hunger,
And choose my dwelling where no Sun dares enter,
So he may be releas'd.

1ST CREDITOR
What meane you sir?

2ND ADUOCATE
Onely your fee againe: ther's so much sayd
Already in this cause, and sayd so well,
That should I onely offer to speake in it,
I should not bee heard, or laught at for it.

1ST CREDITOR
'Tis the first mony aduocate ere gaue backe,
Though hee sayd nothing.

ROCHFORT
Be aduis'd, young Lord,
And well considerate, you throw away
Your liberty, and ioyes of life together:
Your bounty is imployd vpon a subiect
That is not sensible of it, with which, wise man
Neuer abus'd his goodnesse; the great vertues
Of your dead father vindicate themselues,
From these mens malice, and breake ope the prison,
Though it containe his body.

NOUALL SENIOR

Let him alone,
If he loue Lords, a Gods name let him weare 'em,
Prouided these consent.

CHARALOIS
I hope they are not
So ignorant in any way of profit,
As to neglect a possibility
To get their owne, by seeking it from that
Which can returne them nothing, but ill fame,
And curses for their barbarous cruelties.

3RD CREDITOR
What thinke you of the offer?

2ND CREDITOR
Very well.

1ST CREDITOR
Accept it by all meanes: let's shut him vp,
He is well-shaped and has a villanous tongue,
And should he study that way of reuenge,
As I dare almost sweare he loues a wench,
We haue no wiues, nor neuer shall get daughters
That will hold out against him.

Du CROY
What's your answer?

2ND CREDITOR
Speake you for all.

1ST CREDITOR
Why let our executions
That lye vpon the father, bee return'd
Vpon the sonne, and we release the body.

NOUALL SENIOR
The Court must grant you that.

CHARALOIS
I thanke your Lordships,
They haue in it confirm'd on me such glory,
As no time can take from me: I am ready,
Come lead me where you please: captiuity
That comes with honour, is true liberty.

[Exit **CHARMI, CREDITORS** & **OFFICERS**.

NOUALL SENIOR
Strange rashnesse.

ROCHFORT
A braue resolution rather,
Worthy a better fortune, but howeuer
It is not now to be disputed, therefore
To my owne cause. Already I haue found
Your Lordships bountifull in your fauours to me;
And that should teach my modesty to end heere
And presse your loues no further.

Du CROY
There is nothing
The Court can grant, but with assurance you
May aske it and obtaine it.

ROCHFORT
You incourage
A bold Petitioner, and 'tis not fit
Your fauours should be lost. Besides, 'tas beene
A custome many yeeres, at the surrendring
The place I now giue vp, to grant the President
One boone, that parted with it. And to confirme
Your grace towards me, against all such as may
Detract my actions, and life hereafter,
I now preferre it to you.

Du CROY
Speake it freely.

ROCHFORT
I then desire the liberty of Romont,
And that my Lord Nouall, whose priuate wrong
Was equall to the iniurie that was done
To the dignity of the Court, will pardon it,
And now signe his enlargement.

NOUALL SENIOR
Pray you demand
The moyety of my estate, or any thing
Within my power, but this.

ROCHFORT
Am I denyed then—
My first and last request?

Du CROY
It must not be.

2ND PRESIDENT
I haue a voyce to giue in it.

3RD PRESIDENT
And I.
And if perswasion will not worke him to it,
We will make knowne our power.

NOUALL SENIOR
You are too violent,
You shall haue my consent—But would you had
Made tryall of my loue in any thing
But this, you should haue found then—But it skills not.
You haue what you desire.

ROCHFORT
I thanke your Lordships.

Du CROY
The court is vp, make way.

[Exit **OMNES**, praeter **ROCHFORT** & **BAUMONT**.

ROCHFORT
I follow you—Baumont.

BAUMONT
My Lord.

ROCHFORT
You are a scholler, Baumont,
And can search deeper into th' intents of men,
Then those that are lesse knowing—How appear'd
The piety and braue behauior of
Young Charloyes to you?

BAUMONT
It is my wonder,
Since I want language to expresse it fully;
And sure the Collonell—

ROCHFORT
Fie! he was faulty—
What present mony haue I?

BAUMONT
There is no want
Of any summe a priuate man has use for.

ROCHFORT
'Tis well:
I am strangely taken with this Charalois;
Me thinkes, from his example, the whole age
Should learne to be good, and continue so.
Vertue workes strangely with vs: and his goodnesse
Rising aboue his fortune, seemes to me
Princelike, to will, not aske a courtesie.

[Exeunt.

ACT SECONDUS

SCENE I

A Street Before the Prison

Enter **PONTALIER, MALOTIN, BAUMONT**.

MALOTIN
Tis strange.

BAUMONT
Me thinkes so.

PONTALIER
In a man, but young,
Yet old in iudgement, theorique, and practicke
In all humanity (and to increase the wonder)
Religious, yet a Souldier, that he should
Yeeld his free liuing youth a captiue, for
The freedome of his aged fathers Corpes,
And rather choose to want lifes necessaries,
Liberty, hope of fortune, then it should
In death be kept from Christian ceremony.

MALOTIN
Come, 'Tis a golden president in a Sonne,
To let strong nature haue the better hand,
(In such a case) of all affected reason.
What yeeres sits on this Charolois?

BAUMONT
Twenty eight,
For since the clocke did strike him 17 old
Vnder his fathers wing, this Sonne hath fought,
Seru'd and commanded, and so aptly both,
That sometimes he appear'd his fathers father,
And neuer lesse then's sonne; the old man's vertues
So recent in him, as the world may sweare,
Nought but a faire tree, could such fayre fruit beare.

PONTALIER
But wherefore lets he such a barbarous law,
And men more barbarous to execute it,
Preuaile on his soft disposition,
That he had rather dye aliue for debt
Of the old man in prison, then he should
Rob him of Sepulture, considering
These monies borrow'd bought the lenders peace,
And all their meanes they inioy, nor was diffus'd
In any impious or licencious path?

BAUMONT
True: for my part, were it my fathers trunke,
The tyrannous Ram-heads, with their hornes should gore it,
Or, cast it to their curres (than they) lesse currish,
Ere prey on me so, with their Lion-law,
Being in my free will (as in his) to shun it.

PONTALIER
Alasse! he knowes him selfe (in pouerty) lost:
For in this parciall auaricious age
What price beares Honor? Vertue? Long agoe
It was but prays'd, and freez'd, but now a dayes
'Tis colder far, and has, nor loue, nor praise,
Very prayse now freezeth too: for nature
Did make the heathen, far more Christian then,
Then knowledge vs (lesse heathenish) Christian.

MALOTIN
This morning is the funerall.

PONTALIER
Certainely!
And from this prison 'twas the sonnes request
That his deare father might interment haue.

[Recorders Musique,

See, the young sonne interd a liuely graue.

BAUMONT
They come, obserue their order.

[Enter Funerall. Body borne by **4 CAPTAINES** and **SOULDIERS, MOURNERS, SCUTCHIONS**, and very good order. **CHARALOIS**, and **ROMONT** meet it. **CHARALOIS** speaks. **ROMONT** weeping, solemne Musique, **3 CREDITORS**.

CHARALOIS
How like a silent streame shaded with night,
And gliding softly with our windy sighes;
Moues the whole frame of this solemnity!
Teares, sighs, and blackes, filling the simily,
Whilst I the onely murmur in this groue
Of death, thus hollowly break forth! Vouchsafe
To stay a while, rest, rest in peace, deare earth,
Thou that brought'st rest to their vnthankfull lyues,
Whose cruelty deny'd thee rest in death:
Heere stands thy poore Executor thy sonne,
That makes his life prisoner, to bale thy death;
Who gladlier puts on this captiuity,
Then Virgins long in loue, their wedding weeds:
Of all that euer thou hast done good to,
These onely haue good memories, for they
Remember best, forget not gratitude.
I thanke you for this last and friendly loue.
And tho this Country, like a viperous mother,
Not onely hath eate vp vngratefully
All meanes of thee her sonne, but last thy selfe,
Leauing thy heire so bare and indigent,
He cannot rayse thee a poore Monument,
Such as a flatterer, or a vsurer hath.
Thy worth, in euery honest brest buyldes one,
Making their friendly hearts thy funerall stone.

PONTALIER
Sir.

CHARALOIS
Peace, O peace, this sceane is wholy mine.
What weepe ye, souldiers? Blanch not,

[**ROMONT** weepes.

Ha, let me see, my miracle is eas'd,
The iaylors and the creditors do weepe;
Euen they that make vs weepe, do weepe themselues.

Be these thy bodies balme: these and thy vertue
Keepe thy fame euer odoriferous,
Whilst the great, proud, rich, vndeseruing man,
Aliue stinkes in his vices, and being vanish'd,
The golden calfe that was an Idoll dect
With marble pillars let, and Porphyrie,
Shall quickly both in bone and name consume,
Though wrapt in lead, spice, Searecloth and perfume

1ST CREDITOR
Sir.

CHARALOIS
What! Away for shame: you prophane rogues
Must not be mingled with these holy reliques:
This is a Sacrifice, our showre shall crowne
His sepulcher with Oliue, Myrrh and Bayes
The plants of peace, of sorrow, victorie,
Your teares would spring but weedes.

1ST CREDITOR
Would they not so?
Wee'll keepe them to stop bottles then:

ROMONT
No; keepe 'em
For your owne sins, you Rogues, till you repent:
You'll dye else and be damn'd.

2ND CREDITOR
Damn'd, ha! ha, ha.

ROMONT
Laugh yee?

3RD CREDITOR
Yes faith, Sir, weel'd be very glad
To please you eyther way.

1ST CREDITOR
Y'are ne're content,
Crying nor laughing.

ROMONT
Both with a birth shee rogues.

2ND CREDITOR
Our wiues, Sir, taught vs.

ROMONT
Looke, looke, you slaues, your thanklesse cruelty
And sauage manners, of vnkind Dijon,
Exhaust these flouds, and not his fathers death.

1ST CREDITOR
Slid, Sir, what would yee, ye'are so cholericke?

2ND CREDITOR
Most soldiers are so yfaith, let him alone:
They haue little else to liue on, we haue not had
A penny of him, haue we?

3RD CREDITOR
'Slight, wo'd you haue our hearts?

1ST CREDITOR
We haue nothing but his body heere in durance
For all our mony.

PRIEST
On.

CHARALOIS
One moment more,
But to bestow a few poore legacyes,
All I haue left in my dead fathers rights,
And I haue done. Captaine, weare thou these spurs
That yet ne're made his horse runne from a foe.
Lieutenant, thou, this Scarfe, and may it tye
Thy valor, and thy honestie together:
For so it did in him. Ensigne, this Curace
Your Generalls necklace once. You gentle Bearers,
Deuide this purse of gold, this other, strow
Among the poore: tis all I haue. Romont,
(Weare thou this medall of himselfe) that like
A hearty Oake, grew'st close to this tall Pine,
Euen in the wildest wildernese of war,
Whereon foes broke their swords, and tyr'd themselues;
Wounded and hack'd yee were, but neuer fell'd.
For me my portion prouide in Heauen:
My roote is earth'd, and I a desolate branch
Left scattered in the high way of the world,
Trod vnder foot, that might haue bin a Columne,
Mainly supporting our demolish'd house,
This would I weare as my inheritance.
And what hope can arise to me from it,

When I and it are both heere prisoners?
Onely may this, if euer we be free,
Keepe, or redeeme me from all infamie.

[Song. Musicke – A Dirge.

Fie, cease to wonder,
Though you are heare Orpheus with his Iuory Lute,
Moue Trees and Rockes.
Charme Buls, Beares, and men more sauage to be mute,
Weake foolish singer, here is one,
Would haue transform'd thy selfe, to stone.

1ST CREDITOR
No farther, looke to 'em at your owne perill.

2ND CREDITOR
No, as they please: their Master's a good man.
I would they were the Burmudas.

SAYLOR
You must no further.
The prison limits you, and the Creditors
Exact the strictnesse.

ROMONT
Out you wooluish mungrells!
Whose braynes should be knockt out, like dogs in Iuly,
Leste your infection poyson a whole towne.

CHARALOIS
They grudge our sorrow: your ill wills perforce
Turnes now to Charity: they would not haue vs
Walke too farre mourning, vsurers reliefe
Grieues, if the Debtors haue too much of griefe.

[Exeunt.

SCENE II

A Room in Rochfort's House.

[Enter **BEAUMELLE, FLORIMELL, BELLAPERT**.

BEAUMELLE
I prithee tell me, Florimell, why do women marry?

FLORIMELL
Why truly Madam, I thinke, to lye with their husbands.

BELLAPERT
You are a foole: She lyes, Madam, women marry husbands,
To lye with other men.

FLORIMELL
Faith eene such a woman wilt thou make. By this light, Madam, this wagtaile will spoyle you, if you take delight in her licence.

BEAUMELLE
Tis true, Florimell: and thou wilt make me too good for a yong Lady. What an electuary found my father out for his daughter, when hee compounded you two my women? for thou, Florimell, art eene a graine to heauy, simply for a wayting Gentlewoman.

FLORIMELL
And thou Bellapert, a graine too light.

BELLAPERT
Well, go thy wayes goodly wisdom, whom no body regards. I wonder, whether be elder thou or thy hood: you thinke, because you serue my Laydes mother, are 32 yeeres old which is a peepe out, you know.

FLORIMELL
Well sayd, wherligig.

BELLAPERT
You are deceyu'd: I want a peg ith' middle. Out of these Prerogatiues! you thinke to be mother of the maydes heere, & mortifie em with prouerbs: goe, goe, gouern the sweet meates, and waigh the Suger, that the wenches steale none: say your prayers twice a day, and as I take it, you haue performd your function.

FLORIMELL
I may bee euen with you.

BELLAPERT
Harke, the Court's broke vp. Goe helpe my old Lord out of his Caroch, and scratch his head till dinner time.

FLORIMELL
Well.

[Exit.

BELLAPERT

Fy Madam, how you walke! By my mayden-head you looke 7 yeeres older then you did this morning: why, there can be nothing vnder the Sunne vanuable, to make you thus a minute.

BEAUMELLE
Ah my sweete Bellapert thou Cabinet
To all my counsels, thou dost know the cause
That makes thy Lady wither thus in youth.

BELLAPERT
Vd'd-light, enioy your wishes: whilst I liue,
One way or other you shall crowne your will.
Would you haue him your husband that you loue,
And can't not bee? he is your seruant though,
And may performe the office of a husband.

BEAUMELLE
But there is honor, wench.

BELLAPERT
Such a disease
There is in deed, for which ere I would dy.—

BEAUMELLE
Prethee, distinguish me a mayd & wife.

BELLAPERT
Faith, Madam, one may beare any mans children,
Tother must beare no mans.

BEAUMELLE
What is a husband?

BELLAPERT
Physicke, that tumbling in your belly, will make you sicke ith' stomacke: the onely distinction betwixt a husband and a seruant is: the first will lye with you, when he please; the last shall lye with you when you please. Pray tell me, Lady, do you loue, to marry after, or would you marry, to loue after.

BEAUMELLE
I would meete loue and marriage both at once.

BELLAPERT
Why then you are out of the fashion, and wilbe contemn'd; for (Ile assure you) there are few women i'th world, but either they haue married first, and loue after, or loue first, and marryed after: you must do as you may, not as you would: your fathers will is the Goale you must fly to: if a husband approach you, you would haue further off, is he your loue? the lesse neere you. A husband in these days is but a cloake to bee oftner layde vpon your bed, then in your bed.

BEAUMELLE

Humpe.

BELLAPERT
Sometimes you may weare him on your shoulder,
now and then vnder your arme: but seldome or neuer let him
couer you: for 'tis not the fashion.

[Enter **NOUALL JUNIOR**, **PONTALIER, MALOTIN, LILLADAM, AYMER**.

NOUALL JUNIOR
Best day to natures curiosity,
Starre of Dijum, the lustre of all France,
Perpetuall spring dwell on thy rosy cheekes,
Whose breath is perfume to our Continent,
See Flora turn'd in her varieties.

BELLAPERT
Oh diuine Lord!

NOUALL JUNIOR
No autumne, nor no age euer approach
This heauenly piece, which nature hauing wrought,
She lost her needle and did then despaire,
Euer to work so liuely and so faire.

LILLADAM
Vds light, my Lord one of the purles of your band
is (without all discipline falne) out of his ranke.

NOUALL JUNIOR
How? I would not for a 1000 crownes she had seen't.
Deare Liladam, reforme it.

BELLAPERT
O Lord: Per se, Lord, quintessence of honour,
shee walkes not vnder a weede that could deny thee any
thing.

BAUMONT
Prethy peace, wench, thou dost but blow the fire,
that flames too much already.

[**LILLADAM, AYMER** trim **NOUALL JUNIOR**, whilst **BELL** her **LADY**.

AYMER
By gad, my Lord, you haue the diuinest
Taylor of Christendome; he hath made
you looke like an Angell in your cloth of Tissue doublet.

PONTALIER
This is a three-leg'd Lord, ther's a fresh assault, oh
that men should spend time thus!
See see, how her blood driues to her heart, and straight
vaults to her cheekes againe.

MALOTIN
What are these?

PONTALIER
One of 'em there the lower is a good, foolish, knauish sociable gallimaufry of a man, and has much taught my Lord with singing, hee is master of a musicke house: the other is his dressing blocke, vpon whom my Lord layes all his cloathes, and fashions, ere he vouchsafes 'em his owne person; you shall see him i'th morning in the Gally-foyst, at noone in the Bullion, i'th euening in Quirpo, and all night in—

MALOTIN
A Bawdy house.

PONTALIER
If my Lord deny, they deny, if hee affirme, they affirme: they skip into my Lords cast skins some twice a yeere, and thus they liue to eate, eate to liue, and liue to prayfe my Lord.

MALOTIN
Good sir, tell me one thing.

PONTALIER
What's that?

MALOTIN
Dare these men euer fight, on any cause?

PONTALIER
Oh no, 't would spoyle their cloathes, and put their bands out of order.

NOUALL JUNIOR
Mrs, you heare the news: your father has resign'd his Presidentship to my Lord my father.

MALOTIN
And Lord Charolois vndone foreuer.

PONTALIER
Troth, 'tis pity, sir.
A brauer hope of so assur'd a father
Did neuer comfort France.

LILLADAM
A good dumbe mourner.

AYMER
A silent blacke.
As if he had come this Christmas from St. Omers.

NOUALL JUNIOR
Oh fie vpon him, how he weares his cloathes!
To see his friends, and return'd after Twelfetyde.

LILLADAM
His Colonell lookes fienely like a drouer.

NOUALL JUNIOR
That had a winter ly'n perdieu i'th rayne.

AYMER
What, he that weares a clout about his necke,
His cuffes in's pocket, and his heart in's mouth?

NOUALL JUNIOR
Now out vpon him!

BEAUMELLE
Seruant, tye my hand.
How your lips blush, in scorne that they should pay
Tribute to hands, when lips are in the way!

NOUALL JUNIOR
I thus recant, yet now your hand looks white
Because your lips robd it of such a right.
Mounsieur Aymour, I prethy sing the song
Deuoted to my Mrs.

[Cantat. Musicke.

[Second Song.

[A Dialogue betweene **NOUALL JUNIOR** (**Man**), and **BEAUMELLE** (**Woman**).

Man.
Set Phoebus, set, a fayrer sunne doth rise,
From the bright Radience of my Mrs. eyes
Then euer thou begat'st. I dare not looke,
Each haire a golden line, each word a hooke,
The more I striue, the more I still am tooke.

Woman.
Fayre seruant, come, the day these eyes doe lend

To warme thy blood, thou doest so vainely spend.
Come strangled breath.

Man.
What noate so sweet as this,
That calles the spirits to a further blisse?

Woman.
Yet this out-sauours wine, and this Perfume.

Man.
Let's die, I languish, I consume.

[After the Song, Enter **ROCHFORT**, & **BAUMONT**.

BAUMONT
Romont will come, sir, straight.

ROCHFORT
'Tis well.

BEAUMELLE
My Father.

NOUALL JUNIOR
My honorable Lord.

ROCHFORT
My Lord Nouall this is a vertue in you.
So early vp and ready before noone,
That are the map of dressing through all France.

NOUALL JUNIOR
I rise to say my prayers, sir, heere's my Saint.

ROCHFORT
Tis well and courtly; you must giue me leaue,
I haue some priuate conference with my daughter,
Pray vse my garden, you shall dine with me.

LILLADAM
Wee'l waite on you.

NOUALL JUNIOR
Good morne vnto your Lordship,
Remember what you haue vow'd—to his Mrs.

BEAUMELLE

Performe I must.

[Exeunt **OMNES** praeter **ROCHFORT, BEAUMELLE**.

ROCHFORT
Why how now Beaumelle, thou look'st not well.
Th' art sad of late, come cheere thee, I haue found
A wholesome remedy for these mayden fits,
A goodly Oake whereon to twist my vine,
Till her faire branches grow vp to the starres.
Be neere at hand, successe crowne my intent,
My businesse fills my little time so full,
I cannot stand to talke: I know, thy duty
Is handmayd to my will, especially
When it presents nothing but good and fit.

BEAUMELLE
Sir, I am yours. Oh if my teares proue true,

[Exit **BEAUMELLE**.

Fate hath wrong'd loue, and will destroy me too.

[Enter **ROMONT, KEEPER**

ROMONT
Sent you for me, sir?

ROCHFORT
Yes.

ROMONT
Your Lordships pleasure?

ROCHFORT
Keeper, this prisoner I will see forth comming
Vpon my word—Sit downe good Colonell.

[Exit **KEEPER**.

Why I did wish you hither, noble sir,
Is to aduise you from this yron carriage,
Which, so affected, Romont, you weare,
To pity and to counsell yee submit
With expedition to the great Nouall:
Recant your sterne contempt, and slight neglect
Of the whole Court, and him, and opportunity,
Or you will vndergoe a heauy censure

In publique very shortly.

ROMONT
Hum hum: reuerend sir,
I haue obseru'd you, and doe know you well,
And am now more affraid you know not me,
By wishing my submission to Nouall,
Then I can be of all the bellowing mouthes
That waite vpon him to pronounce the censure,
Could it determine me torments, and shame.
Submit, and craue forgiuenesse of a beast?
Tis true, this bile of state weares purple Tissue.
Is high fed, proud: so is his Lordships horse,
And beares as rich Caparisons. I know,
This Elephant carries on his back not onely
Towres, Castles, but the ponderous republique,
And neuer stoops for't, with his strong breath trunk
Snuffes others titles, Lordships, Offices,
Wealth, bribes, and lyues, vnder his rauenous iawes.
Whats this vnto my freedome? I dare dye;
And therefore aske this Cammell, if these blessings
(For so they would be vnderstood by a man)
But mollifie one rudenesse in his nature,
Sweeten the eager relish of the law,
At whose great helme he sits: helps he the poore
In a iust businesse? nay, does he not crosse
Euery deserued souldier and scholler,
As if when nature made him, she had made
The generall Antipathy of all vertue?
How sauagely, and blasphemously hee spake
Touching the Generall, the graue Generall dead,
I must weepe when I thinke on't.

ROCHFORT
Sir

ROMONT
My Lord,
I am not stubborne, I can melt, you see,
And prize a vertue better then my life:
For though I be not learnd, I euer lou'd
That holy Mother of all issues, good,
Whose white hand (for a Scepter) holds a File
To pollish roughest customes, and in you
She has her right: see, I am calme as sleepe,
But when I thinke of the grosse iniuries
The godlesse wrong done, to my Generall dead,
I raue indeed, and could eate this Nouall

A Isoule-esse Dromodary.

ROCHFORT
Oh bee temperate,
Sir, though I would perswade, I'le not constraine:
Each mans opinion freely is his owne,
Concerning any thing or any body,
Be it right or wrong, tis at the Iudges perill.

[Enter **BAUMONT**,

BAUMONT
These men, Sir, waite without, my Lord is come too.

ROCHFORT
Pay 'em those summes vpon the table, take
Their full releases: stay, I want a witnesse:
Let mee intreat you Colonell, to walke in,
And stand but by, to see this money pay'd,
It does concerne you and your friends, it was
The better cause you were sent for, though sayd otherwise.
The deed shall make this my request more plaine.

ROMONT
I shall obey your pleasure Sir, though ignorant
To what is tends?

[Exit **SERVANT, ROMONT**. Enter **CHARALOIS**.

ROCHFORT
Worthiest Sir,
You are most welcome: fye, no more of this:
You haue out-wept a woman, noble Charolois.
No man but has, or must bury a father.

CHARALOIS
Graue Sir, I buried sorrow, for his death,
In the graue with him. I did neuer thinke
Hee was immortall, though I vow I grieue,
And see no reason why the vicious,
Vertuous, valiant and vnworthy man
Should dye alike.

ROCHFORT
They do not.

CHARALOIS
In the manner

Of dying, Sir, they do not, but all dye,
And therein differ not: but I haue done.
I spy'd the liuely picture of my father,
Passing your gallery, and that cast this water
Into mine eyes: see, foolish that I am,
To let it doe so.

ROCHFORT
Sweete and gentle nature,
How silken is this well comparatiuely
To other men! I haue a suite to you Sir.

CHARALOIS
Take it, tis granted.

ROCHFORT
What?

CHARALOIS
Nothing, my Lord.

ROCHFORT
Nothing is quickly granted.

CHARALOIS
Faith, my Lord,
That nothing granted, is euen all I haue,
For (all know) I haue nothing left to grant.

ROCHFORT
Sir, ha' you any suite to me? Ill grant
You something, any thing.

CHARALOIS
Nay surely, I that can
Giue nothing, will but sue for that againe.
No man will grant mee any thing I sue for.
But begging nothing, euery man will giue't.

ROCHFORT
Sir, the loue I bore your father, and the worth
I see in you, so much resembling his.
Made me thus send for you. And tender heere

[Drawes a Curtayne.

What euer you will take, gold, Iewels, both,
All, to supply your wants, and free your selfe.

Where heauenly vertue in high blouded veines
Is lodg'd, and can agree, men should kneele downe,
Adore, and sacrifice all that they haue;
And well they may, it is so seldome seene.
Put off your wonder, and heere freely take
Or send your seruants. Nor, Sir, shall you vse
In ought of this, a poore mans fee, or bribe,
Vniustly taken of the rich, but what's
Directly gotten, and yet by the Law.

CHARALOIS
How ill, Sir, it becomes those haires to mocke?

ROCHFORT
Mocke? thunder strike mee then.

CHARALOIS
You doe amaze mee:
But you shall wonder too, I will not take
One single piece of this great heape: why should I
Borrow, that haue not meanes to pay, nay am
A very bankerupt, euen in flattering hope
Of euer raysing any. All my begging,
Is Romonts libertie.

[Enter **ROMONT. CREDITORS** loaden with mony. **BAUMONT**.

ROCHFORT
Heere is your friend,
Enfranchist ere you spake. I giue him you,
And Charolois. I giue you to your friend
As free a man as hee; your fathers debts
Are taken off.

CHARALOIS
How?

ROMONT
Sir, it is most true.
I am the witnes.

1ST CREDITOR
Yes faith, wee are pay'd.

2ND CREDITOR
Heauen blesse his Lordship, I did thinke him wiser.

3RD CREDITOR

He a states-man, he an asse Pay other mens debts?

1ST CREDITOR
That he was neuer bound for.

ROMONT
One more such
Would saue the rest of pleaders.

CHARALOIS
Honord Rochfort.
Lye still my toung and bushes, cal'd my cheekes,
That offter thankes in words, for such great deeds.

ROCHFORT
Call in my daughter: still I haue a suit to you.

[Exit **BAUMONT**.

Would you requite mee.

ROMONT
With his life, assure you.

ROCHFORT
Nay, would you make me now your debter, Sir.
This is my onely child: what shee appeares,

[Enter **BAUMONT, BEAUMELLE**.

Your Lordship well may see her education
Followes not any: for her mind, I know it
To be far fayrer then her shape, and hope
It will continue so: if now her birth
Be not too meane for Charolois, take her
This virgin by the hand, and call her wife,
Indowd with all my fortunes: blesse me so,
Requite mee thus, and make mee happier,
In ioyning my poore empty name to yours,
Then if my state were multiplied ten fold.

CHARALOIS
Is this the payment, Sir, that you expect?
Why, you participate me more in debt,
That nothing but my life can euer pay,
This beautie being your daughter, in which yours
I must conceiue necessitie of her vertue
Without all dowry is a Princes ayme,

Then, as shee is, for poore and worthlesse I,
How much too worthy! Waken me, Romont,
That I may know I dream't and find this vanisht

ROMONT
Sure, I sleepe not.

ROCHFORT
Your sentence life or death.

CHARALOIS
Faire Beaumelle, can you loue me?

BEAUMELLE
Yes, my Lord.

[Enter **NOUALL JUNIOR**, **PONTALIER**, **MALOTIN, LILLADAM, AYMER**. All salute

CHARALOIS
You need not question me, if I can you.
You are the fayrest virgin in Digum,
And Rochfort is your father.

NOUALL JUNIOR
What's this change?

ROCHFORT
You met my wishes, Gentlemen.

ROMONT
What make
These dogs in doublets heere?

BEAUMELLE
A Visitation, Sir.

CHARALOIS
Then thus, Faire Beaumelle, I write my faith
Thus seale it in the sight of Heauen and men.
Your fingers tye my heart-strings with this touch
In true-loue knots, which nought but death shall loose.
And yet these eares (an Embleme of our loues)
Like Cristall riuers indiuidually
Flow into one another, make one source,
Which neuer man distinguish, lesse deuide:
Breath, marry, breath, and kisses, mingle soules
Two hearts, and bodies, heere incorporate:
And though with little wooing I haue wonne

My future life shall be a wooing tyme.
And euery day, new as the bridall one.
Oh Sir I groane vnder your courtesies,
More then my fathers bones vnder his wrongs,
You Curtius-like, haue throwne into the gulfe,
Of this his Countries foule ingratitude,
Your life and fortunes, to redeeme their shames.

ROCHFORT
No more, my glory, come, let's in and hasten
This celebration.

ROMONT, MALOTIN, PONTALIER, BAUMONT
All faire blisse vpon it.

[Exeunt **ROCHFORT, CHARALOIS**, **ROMONT, BAUMONT, MALOTIN**.

NOUALL JUNIOR
Mistresse.

BEAUMELLE
Oh seruant, vertue strengthen me.
Thy presence blowes round my affections vane:
You will vndoe me, if you speake againe.

[Exit **BEAUMELLE**.

LILLADAM, AYMER
Heere will be sport for you. This workes.

[Exeunt **LILLADAM, AYMER**.

NOUALL JUNIOR
Peace, peace,

PONTALIER
One word, my Lord Nouall.

NOUALL JUNIOR
What, thou wouldst mony; there.

PONTALIER
No, Ile none, Ile not be bought a slaue,
A Pander, or a Parasite, for all
Your fathers worth, though you haue sau'd my life,
Rescued me often from my wants, I must not
Winke at your follyes: that will ruine you.
You know my blunt way, and my loue to truth:

Forsake the pursuit of this Ladies honour,
Now you doe see her made another mans,
And such a mans, so good, so popular,
Or you will plucke a thousand mischiefes on you.
The benefits you haue done me, are not lost,
Nor cast away, they are purs'd heere in my heart,
But let me pay you, sir, a fayrer way
Then to defend your vices, or to sooth 'em.

NOUALL JUNIOR
Ha, ha, ha, what are my courses vnto thee?
Good Cousin Pontalier, meddle with that
That shall concerne thyselfe.

[Exit **NOUALL JUNIOR**.

PONTALIER
No more but scorne?
Moue on then, starres, worke your pernicious will.
Onely the wise rule, and preuent your ill.

[Exit. **HOBOYES**.

Here a passage ouer the Stage, while the Act is playing for the Marriage of **CHARALOIS** with **BEAUMELLE**, &c.

ACTUS TERTIUS

SCENE I

A Room in Charalois' House

Enter **NOUALL JUNIOR, BELLAPERT**.

NOUALL JUNIOR
Flie not to these excuses: thou hast bin
False in thy promise, and when I haue said
Vngratefull, all is spoke.

BELLAPERT
Good my Lord,
But heare me onely.

NOUALL JUNIOR
To what purpose, trifler?

Can anything that thou canst say, make voyd
The marriage? or those pleasures but a dreame,
Which Charalois (oh Venus) hath enioyd?

BELLAPERT
I yet could say that you receiue aduantage,
In what you thinke a losse, would you vouchsafe me
That you were neuer in the way till now
With safety to arriue at your desires,
That pleasure makes loue to you vnattended
By danger or repentance?

NOUALL JUNIOR
That I could.
But apprehend one reason how this might be,
Hope would not then forsake me.

BELLAPERT
The enioying
Of what you most desire, I say th' enioying
Shall, in the full possession of your wishes,
Confirme that I am faithfull.

NOUALL JUNIOR
Giue some rellish
How this may appeare possible.

BELLAPERT
I will
Rellish, and taste, and make the banquet easie:
You say my Ladie's married. I confesse it,
That Charalois hath inioyed her, 'tis most true
That with her, hee's already Master of
The best part of my old Lords state. Still better,
But that the first, or last, should be your hindrance,
I vtterly deny: for but obserue me:
While she went for, and was, I sweare, a Virgin,
What courtesie could she with her honour giue
Or you receiue with safety—take me with you,
When I say courtesie, doe not think I meane
A kisse, the tying of her shoo or garter,
An houre of priuate conference: those are trifles.
In this word courtesy, we that are gamesters point at
The sport direct, where not alone the louer
Brings his Artillery, but vses it.
Which word expounded to you, such a courtesie
Doe you expect, and sudden.

NOUALL JUNIOR
But he tasted
The first sweetes, Bellapert.

BELLAPERT
He wrong'd you shrewdly,
He toyl'd to climbe vp to the Phoenix nest,
And in his prints leaues your ascent more easie.
I doe not know, you that are perfect Crittiques
In womens bookes, may talke of maydenheads.

NOUALL JUNIOR
But for her marriage.

BELLAPERT
'Tis a faire protection
'Gainst all arrests of feare, or shame for euer.
Such as are faire, and yet not foolish, study
To haue one at thirteene; but they are mad
That stay till twenty. Then sir, for the pleasure,
To say Adulterie's sweeter, that is stale.
This onely is not the contentment more,
To say, This is my Cuckold, then my Riuall.
More I could say—but briefly, she doates on you,
If it proue otherwise, spare not, poyson me
With the next gold you giue me.

[Enter **BEAUMELLE.**

BEAUMELLE
Hows this seruant,
Courting my woman?

BELLAPERT
As an entrance to
The fauour of the mistris: you are together
And I am perfect in my qu.

BEAUMELLE
Stay Bellapert.

BELLAPERT
In this I must not with your leaue obey you.
Your Taylor and your Tire-woman waite without
And stay my counsayle, and direction for
Your next dayes dressing. I haue much to doe,
Nor will your Ladiship know, time is precious,
Continue idle: this choise Lord will finde

So fit imployment for you.

[Exit **BELLAPERT**.

BEAUMELLE
I shall grow angry.

NOUALL JUNIOR
Not so, you haue a iewell in her, Madam.

[Enter againe.

BELLAPERT
I had forgot to tell your Ladiship
The closet is priuate and your couch ready:
And if you please that I shall loose the key,
But say so, and tis done.

[Exit **BELLAPERT**.

BAUMONT
You come to chide me, seruant, and bring with you
Sufficient warrant, you will say and truely,
My father found too much obedience in me,
By being won too soone: yet if you please
But to remember, all my hopes and fortunes
Had reuerence to this likening: you will grant
That though I did not well towards you, I yet
Did wisely for my selfe.

NOUALL JUNIOR
With too much feruor
I haue so long lou'd and still loue you, Mistresse,
To esteeme that an iniury to me
Which was to you conuenient: that is past
My helpe, is past my cure. You yet may, Lady,
In recompence of all my dutious seruice,
(Prouided that your will answere your power)
Become my Creditresse.

BEAUMELLE
I vnderstand you,
And for assurance, the request you make
Shall not be long vnanswered. Pray you sit,
And by what you shall heare, you'l easily finde,
My passions are much fitter to desire,
Then to be sued to.

[Enter **ROMONT** and **FLORIMELL**.

FLORIMELL
Sir, tis not enuy
At the start my fellow has got of me in
My Ladies good opinion, thats the motiue
Of this discouery; but due payment
Of what I owe her Honour.

ROMONT
So I conceiue it.

FLORIMELL
I haue obserued too much, nor shall my silence
Preuent the remedy—yonder they are,
I dare not bee seene with you. You may doe
What you thinke fit, which wil be, I presume,
The office of a faithfull and tryed friend
To my young Lord.

[Exit **FLORIMELL**.

ROMONT
This is no vision: ha!

NOUALL JUNIOR
With the next opportunity.

BEAUMELLE
By this kisse,
And this, and this.

NOUALL JUNIOR
That you would euer sweare thus.

ROMONT
If I seeme rude, your pardon, Lady; yours
I do not aske: come, do not dare to shew mee
A face of anger, or the least dislike.
Put on, and suddaily a milder looke,
I shall grow rough else.

NOUALL JUNIOR
What haue I done, Sir,
To draw this harsh vnsauory language from you?

ROMONT
Done, Popinjay? why, dost thou thinke that if

I ere had dreamt that thou hadst done me wrong,
Thou shouldest outliue it?

BEAUMELLE
This is something more
Then my Lords friendship giues commission for.

NOUALL JUNIOR
Your presence and the place, makes him presume
Vpon my patience.

ROMONT
As if thou ere wer't angry
But with thy Taylor, and yet that poore shred
Can bring more to the making vp of a man,
Then can be hop'd from thee: thou art his creature,
And did hee not each morning new create thee
Thou wouldst stinke and be forgotten. Ile not change
On syllable more with thee, vntill thou bring
Some testimony vnder good mens hands,
Thou art a Christian. I suspect thee strongly,
And wilbe satisfied: till which time, keepe from me.
The entertaiment of your visitation
Has made what I intended on a businesse.

NOUALL JUNIOR
So wee shall meete—Madam.

ROMONT
Vse that legge again,
And Ile cut off the other.

NOUALL JUNIOR
Very good.

[Exit **NOUALL JUNIOR**.

ROMONT
What a perfume the Muske-cat leaues behind him!
Do you admit him for a property,
To saue you charges, Lady.

BEAUMELLE
Tis not vselesse,
Now you are to succeed him.

ROMONT
So I respect you,

Not for your selfe, but in remembrance of,
Who is your father, and whose wife you now are,
That I choose rather not to vnderstand
Your nasty scoffe then,—

BEAUMELLE
What, you will not beate mee,
If I expound it to you. Heer's a Tyrant
Spares neyther man nor woman.

ROMONT
My intents
Madam, deserue not this; nor do I stay
To be the whetstone of your wit: preserue it
To spend on such, as know how to admire
Such coloured stuffe. In me there is now speaks to you
As true a friend and seruant to your Honour,
And one that will with as much hazzard guard it,
As euer man did goodnesse.—But then Lady,
You must endeauour not alone to bee,
But to appeare worthy such loue and seruice.

BEAUMELLE
To what tends this?

ROMONT
Why, to this purpose, Lady,
I do desire you should proue such a wife
To Charalois (and such a one hee merits)
As Caesar, did hee liue, could not except at,
Not onely innocent from crime, but free
From all taynt and suspition.

BEAUMELLE
They are base
That iudge me otherwise.

ROMONT
But yet bee carefull.
Detraction's a bold monster, and feares not
To wound the fame of Princes, if it find
But any blemish in their liues to worke on.
But Ile bee plainer with you: had the people
Bin learnd to speake, but what euen now I saw,
Their malice out of that would raise an engine
To ouerthrow your honor. In my fight
(With yonder pointed foole I frighted from you)
You vs'd familiarity beyond

A modest entertaynment: you embrac'd him
With too much ardor for a stranger, and
Met him with kisses neyther chaste nor comely:
But learne you to forget him, as I will
Your bounties to him, you will find it safer
Rather to be vncourtly, then immodest.

BEAUMELLE
This prety rag about your necke shews well,
And being coorse and little worth, it speakes you,
As terrible as thrifty.

ROMONT
Madam.

BEAUMELLE
Yes.
And this strong belt in which you hang your honor
Will out-last twenty scarfs.

ROMONT
What meane you, Lady?

BEAUMELLE
And all else about you Cap a pe
So vniforme in spite of handsomnesse,
Shews such a bold contempt of comelinesse,
That tis not strange your Laundresse in the League,
Grew mad with loue of you.

ROMONT
Is my free counsayle
Answerd with this ridiculous scorne?

BEAUMELLE
These obiects
Stole very much of my attention from me,
Yet something I remember, to speake truth,
Deceyued grauely, but to little purpose,
That almost would haue made me sweare, some Curate
Had stolne into the person of Romont,
And in the praise of goodwife honesty,
Had read an homely.

ROMONT
By thy hand.

BEAUMELLE

And sword,
I will make vp your oath, twill want weight else.
You are angry with me, and poore I laugh at it.
Do you come from the Campe, which affords onely
The conuersation of cast suburbe whores,
To set downe to a Lady of my ranke,
Lymits of entertainment?

ROMONT
Sure a Legion has possest this woman.

BEAUMELLE
One stampe more would do well: yet I desire not
You should grow horne-mad, till you haue a wife.
You are come to warme meate, and perhaps cleane linnen:
Feed, weare it, and bee thankefull. For me, know,
That though a thousand watches were set on mee,
And you the Master-spy, I yet would vse,
The liberty that best likes mee. I will reuell,
Feast, kisse, imbreace, perhaps grant larger fauours:
Yet such as liue vpon my meanes, shall know
They must not murmur at it. If my Lord
Bee now growne yellow, and has chose out you
To serue his Iealouzy that way, tell him this,
You haue something to informe him:

[Exit **BEAUMELLE**.

ROMONT
And I will.
Beleeue it wicked one I will. Heare, Heauen,
But hearing pardon mee: if these fruts grow
Vpon the tree of marriage, let me shun it,
As a forbidden sweete. An heyre and rich,
Young, beautifull, yet adde to this a wife,
And I will rather choose a Spittle sinner
Carted an age before, though three parts rotten,
And take it for a blessing, rather then
Be fettered to the hellish slauery
Of such an impudence.

[Enter **BAUMONT** with writings.

BAUMONT
Collonell, good fortune
To meet you thus: you looke sad, but Ile tell you
Something that shall remoue it. Oh how happy
Is my Lord Charaloys in his faire bride!

ROMONT
A happy man indeede!—pray you in what?

BAUMONT
I dare sweare, you would thinke so good a Lady,
A dower sufficient.

ROMONT
No doubt. But on.

BAUMONT
So faire, so chaste, so vertuous: so indeed
All that is excellent.

ROMONT
Women haue no cunning
To gull the world.

BAUMONT
Yet to all these, my Lord
Her father giues the full addition of
All he does now possesse in Burgundy:
These writings to confirme it, are new seal'd
And I most fortunate to present him with them,
I must goe seeke him out, can you direct mee?

ROMONT
You'l finde him breaking a young horse.

BAUMONT
I thanke you.

[Exit **BAUMONT**.

ROMONT
I must do something worthy Charaloys friendship.
If she were well inclin'd to keepe her so,
Deseru'd not thankes: and yet to stay a woman
Spur'd headlong by hot lust, to her owne ruine,
Is harder then to prop a falling towre
With a deceiuing reed.

[Enter **ROCHFORT**.

ROCHFORT
Some one seeke for me,
As soone as he returnes.

ROMONT
Her father! ha?
How if I breake this to him? sure it cannot
Meete with an ill construction. His wisedome
Made powerfull by the authority of a father,
Will warrant and giue priuiledge to his counsailes.
It shall be so—my Lord.

ROCHFORT
Your friend Romont:
Would you ought with me?

ROMONT
I stand so engag'd
To your so many fauours, that I hold it
A breach in thankfulnesse, should I not discouer,
Though with some imputation to my selfe,
All doubts that may concerne you.

ROCHFORT
The performance
Will make this protestation worth my thanks.

ROMONT
Then with your patience lend me your attention
For what I must deliuer, whispered onely
You will with too much griefe receiue.

[Enter **BEAUMELLE, BELLAPERT**.

BEAUMELLE
See wench!
Vpon my life as I forespake, hee's now
Preferring his complaint: but be thou perfect,
And we will fit him.

BELLAPERT
Feare not mee, pox on him:
A Captaine turne Informer against kissing?
Would he were hang'd vp in his rusty Armour:
But if our fresh wits cannot turne the plots
Of such a mouldy murrion on it selfe;
Rich cloathes, choyse faire, and a true friend at a call,
With all the pleasures the night yeelds, forsake vs.

ROCHFORT
This in my daughter? doe not wrong her.

BELLAPERT
Now.
Begin. The games afoot, and wee in distance.

BEAUMELLE
Tis thy fault, foolish girle, pinne on my vaile,
I will not weare those iewels. Am I not
Already matcht beyond my hopes? yet still
You prune and set me forth, as if I were
Againe to please a suyter.

BELLAPERT
Tis the course
That our great Ladies take.

ROMONT
A weake excuse.

BEAUMELLE
Those that are better seene, in what concernes
A Ladies honour and faire same, condemne it.
You waite well, in your absence, my Lords friend
The vnderstanding, graue and wise Romont.

ROMONT
Must I be still her sport?

BEAUMELLE
Reproue me for it.
And he has traueld to bring home a iudgement
Not to be contradicted. You will say
My father, that owes more to yeeres then he,
Has brought me vp to musique, language, Courtship,
And I must vse them. True, but not t'offend,
Or render me suspected.

ROCHFORT
Does your fine story
Begin from this?

BEAUMELLE
I thought a parting kisse
From young Nouall, would haue displeasd no more
Then heretofore it hath done; but I finde
I must restrayne such fauours now; looke therefore
As you are carefull to continue mine,
That I no more be visited. Ile endure

The strictest course of life that iealousie
Can thinke secure enough, ere my behauiour
Shall call my fame in question.

ROMONT
Ten dissemblers
Are in this subtile deuill. You beleeue this?

ROCHFORT
So farre that if you trouble me againe
With a report like this, I shall not onely
Iudge you malicious in your disposition,
But study to repent what I haue done
To such a nature.

ROMONT
Why, 'tis exceeding well.

ROCHFORT
And for you, daughter, off with this, off with it:
I haue that confidence in your goodnesse, I,
That I will not consent to haue you liue
Like to a Recluse in a cloyster: goe
Call in the gallants, let them make you merry,
Vse all fit liberty.

BELLAPERT
Blessing on you.
If this new preacher with the sword and feather
Could proue his doctrine for Canonicall,
We should haue a fine world.

[Exit **BELLAPERT**.

ROCHFORT
Sir, if you please
To beare your selfe as fits a Gentleman,
The house is at your seruice: but if not,
Though you seeke company else where, your absence
Will not be much lamented—

[Exit **ROCHFORT**.

ROMONT
If this be
The recompence of striuing to preserue
A wanton gigglet honest, very shortly
'Twill make all mankinde Panders—Do you smile,

Good Lady Loosenes? your whole sex is like you,
And that man's mad that seekes to better any:
What new change haue you next?

BEAUMELLE
Oh, feare not you, sir,
Ile shift into a thousand, but I will
Conuert your heresie.

ROMONT
What heresie? Speake.

BEAUMELLE
Of keeping a Lady that is married,
From entertayning seruants.—

[Enter **NOUALL JUNIOR, MALOTIN, LILLADAM, AYMER, PONTALIER**.

O, you are welcome,
Vae any meanes to vexe him,
And then with welcome follow me.

[Exit **BEAUMELLE**.

NOUALL JUNIOR
You are tyr'd
With your graue exhortations, Collonell.

LILLADAM
How is it? Fayth, your Lordship may doe well,
To helpe him to some Church-preferment: 'tis
Now the fashion, for men of all conditions,
How euer they haue liu'd; to end that way.

AYMER
That face would doe well in a surplesse.

ROMONT
Rogues,
Be silent—or—

PONTALIER
S'death will you suffer this?

ROMONT
And you, the master Rogue, the coward rascall,
I shall be with you suddenly.

NOUALL JUNIOR
Pontallier,
If I should strike him, I know I shall kill him:
And therefore I would haue thee beate him, for
Hee's good for nothing else.

LILLADAM
His backe
Appeares to me, as it would tire a Beadle,
And then he has a knotted brow, would bruise
A courtlike hand to touch it.

AYMER
Hee lookes like
A Curryer when his hides grown deare.

PONTALIER
Take heede
He curry not some of you.

NOUALL JUNIOR
Gods me, hee's angry.

ROMONT
I breake no Iests, but I can breake my sword
About your pates.

[Enter **CHARALOIS** and **BAUMONT**.

LILLADAM
Heeres more.

AYMER
Come let's bee gone,
Wee are beleaguerd.

NOUALL JUNIOR
Looke they bring vp their troups.

PONTALIER
Will you sit downe
With this disgrace? You are abus'd most grosely.

LILLADAM
I grant you, Sir, we are, and you would haue vs
Stay and be more abus'd.

NOUALL JUNIOR

My Lord, I am sorry,
Your house is so inhospitable, we must quit it.

[Exeunt. Manent. **CHARALOIS, ROMONT**.

CHARALOIS
Prethee Romont, what caus'd this vprore?

ROMONT
Nothing.
They laugh'd and vs'd their scuruy wits vpon mee.

CHARALOIS
Come, tis thy Iealous nature: but I wonder
That you which are an honest man and worthy,
Should softer this suspition: no man laughes;
No one can whisper, but thou apprehend'st
His conference and his scorne reflects on thee:
For my part they should scoffe their thin wits out,
So I not heard 'em, beate me, not being there.
Leaue, leaue these fits, to conscious men, to such
As are obnoxious, to those foolish things
As they can gibe at.

ROMONT
Well, Sir.

CHARALOIS
Thou art know'n
Valiant without detect, right defin'd
Which is (as fearing to doe iniury,
As tender to endure it) not a brabbler,
A swearer.

ROMONT
Pish, pish, what needs this my Lord?
If I be knowne none such, how vainly, you
Do cast away good counsaile? I haue lou'd you,
And yet must freely speake; so young a tutor,
Fits not so old a Souldier as I am.
And I must tell you, t'was in your behalfe
I grew inraged thus, yet had rather dye,
Then open the great cause a syllable further.

CHARALOIS
In my behalfe? wherein hath Charalois
Vnfitly so demean'd himselfe, to giue
The least occasion to the loosest tongue,

To throw aspersions on him, or so weakely
Protected his owne honor, as it should
Need a defence from any but himselfe?
They are fools that iudge me by my outward seeming,
Why should my gentlenesse beget abuse?
The Lion is not angry that does sleepe
Nor euery man a Coward that can weepe.
For Gods sake speake the cause.

ROMONT
Not for the world.
Oh it will strike disease into your bones
Beyond the cure of physicke, drinke your blood,
Rob you of all your rest, contract your sight,
Leaue you no eyes but to see misery,
And of your owne, nor speach but to wish thus
Would I had perish'd in the prisons iawes:
From whence I was redeem'd! twill weare you old,
Before you haue experience in that Art,
That causes your affliction.

CHARALOIS
Thou dost strike
A deathfull coldnesse to my hearts high heate,
And shrinkst my liuer like the Calenture.
Declare this foe of mine, and lifes, that like
A man I may encounter and subdue it
It shall not haue one such effect in mee,
As thou denouncest: with a Souldiers arme,
If it be strength, Ile meet it: if a fault
Belonging to my mind, Ile cut it off
With mine owne reason, as a Scholler should
Speake, though it make mee monstrous.

ROMONT
Ile dye first.
Farewell, continue merry, and high Heauen
Keepe your wife chaste.

CHARALOIS
Hump, stay and take this wolfe
Out of my brest, that thou hast lodg'd there, or
For euer lose mee.

ROMONT
Lose not, Sir, your selfe.
And I will venture—So the dore is fast.

[Locke the dore.

Now noble Charaloys, collect your selfe,
Summon your spirits, muster all your strength
That can belong to man, sift passion,
From euery veine, and whatsoeuer ensues,
Vpbraid not me heereafter, as the cause of
Iealousy, discontent, slaughter and ruine:
Make me not parent to sinne: you will know
This secret that I burne with.

CHARALOIS
Diuell on't,
What should it be? Romont, I heare you wish
My wifes continuance of Chastity.

ROMONT
There was no hurt in that.

CHARALOIS
Why? do you know
A likelyhood or possibility vnto the contrarie?

ROMONT
I know it not, but doubt it, these the grounds
The seruant of your wife now young Nouall,
The sonne vnto your fathers Enemy
(Which aggrauates my presumption the more)
I haue been warnd of, touching her, nay, seene them
Tye heart to heart, one in anothers armes,
Multiplying kisses, as if they meant
To pose Arithmeticke, or whose eyes would
Bee first burnt out, with gazing on the others.
I saw their mouthes engender, and their palmes
Glew'd, as if Loue had lockt them, their words flow
And melt each others, like two circling flames,
Where chastity, like a Phoenix (me thought) burn'd,
But left the world nor ashes, nor an heire.
Why stand you silent thus? what cold dull flegme,
As if you had no drop of choller mixt
In your whole constitution, thus preuailes,
To fix you now, thus stupid hearing this?

CHARALOIS
You did not see 'em on my Couch within,
Like George a horse-backe on her, nor a bed?

ROMONT

Noe.

CHARALOIS
Ha, ha.

ROMONT
Laugh yee? eene so did your wife,
And her indulgent father.

CHARALOIS
They were wife.
Wouldst ha me be a foole?

ROMONT
No, but a man.

CHARALOIS
There is no dramme of manhood to suspect,
On such thin ayrie circumstance as this
Meere complement and courtship. Was this tale
The hydeous monster which you so conceal'd?
Away, thou curious impertinent
And idle searcher of such leane nice toyes.
Goe, thou sedicious sower of debate:
Fly to such matches, where the bridegroome doubts:
He holds not worth enough to counteruaile
The vertue and the beauty of his wife.
Thou buzzing drone that 'bout my eares dost hum,
To strike thy rankling sting into my heart,
Whose vemon, time, nor medicine could asswage.
Thus doe I put thee off, and confident
In mine owne innocency, and desert,
Dare not conceiue her so vnreasonable,
To put Nouall in ballance against me,
An vpstart cran'd vp to the height he has.
Hence busiebody, thou'rt no friend to me,
That must be kept to a wiues iniury,

ROMONT
Ist possible? farewell, fine, honest man,
Sweet temper'd Lord adieu: what Apoplexy
Hath knit fence vp? Is this Romonts reward?
Beare witnes the great spirit of my father,
With what a healthfull hope I administer
This potion that hath wrought so virulently,
I not accuse thy wife of act, but would
Preuent her Praecipuce, to thy dishonour,
Which now thy tardy sluggishnesse will admit.

Would I had seene thee grau'd with thy great Sire,
Ere liue to haue mens marginall fingers point
At Charaloys, as a lamented story.
An Emperour put away his wife for touching
Another man, but thou wouldst haue thine tasted
And keepe her (I thinke.) Puffe. I am a fire
To warme a dead man, that waste out myselfe.
Bleed—what a plague, a vengeance i'st to mee,
If you will be a Cuckold? Heere I shew
A swords point to thee, this side you may shun,
Or that: the perrill, if you will runne on,
I cannot helpe it.

CHARALOIS
Didst thou neuer see me
Angry, Romont?

ROMONT
Yes, and pursue a foe
Like lightening

CHARALOIS
Prethee see me so no more.
I can be so againe. Put vp thy sword,
And take thy selfe away, lest I draw mine.

ROMONT
Come fright your foes with this: sir, I am your friend,
And dare stand by you thus.

CHARALOIS
Thou art not my friend,
Or being so, thou art mad, I must not buy
Thy friendship at this rate; had I iust cause,
Thou knowst I durst pursue such iniury
Through fire, ayre, water, earth, nay, were they all
Shuffled againe to Chaos, but ther's none.
Thy skill, Romont, consists in camps, not courts.
Farewell, vnciuill man, let's meet no more.
Heere our long web of friendship I vntwist.
Shall I goe whine, walke pale, and locke my wife
For nothing, from her births free liberty,
That open'd mine to me? yes; if I doe
The name of cuckold then, dog me with scorne.
I am a Frenchman, no Italian borne.

[Exit.

ROMONT
A dull Dutch rather: fall and coole (my blood)
Boyle not in zeal of thy friends hurt, so high,
That is so low, and cold himselfe in't. Woman,
How strong art thou, how easily beguild?
How thou dost racke vs by the very hornes?
Now wealth I see change manners and the man:
Something I must doe mine owne wrath to asswage,
And note my friendship to an after-age.

[Exit.

ACTUS QUARTUS

SCENE I

A Room in Nouall's House

Enter **NOUALL JUNIOR**, as newly dressed, a **TAYLOR, BARBER, PERFUMER, LILLADAM, AYMER, PAGE**.

NOUALL JUNIOR
Mend this a little: pox! thou hast burnt me. oh fie
vpon't, O Lard, hee has made me smell (for
all the world) like a flaxe, or a red headed womans chamber:
powder, powder, powder.

PERFUMER
Oh sweet Lord!

[**NOUALL JUNIOR** sits in a chaire,

PAGE
That's his Perfumer.

[**BARBER** orders his haire,

TAYLOR
Oh deare Lord,

[**PERFUMER** giues powder,

PAGE
That's his Taylor.

[**TAYLOR** sets his clothese.

NOUALL JUNIOR
Monsieur Lilladam, Aymer, how allow you the modell of these clothes?

AYMER
Admirably, admirably, oh sweet Lord! Assuredly it's pity the wormes should eate thee.

PAGE
Here's a fine Cell; a Lord, a Taylor, a Perfumer, a Barber, and a paire of Mounsieurs: 3 to 3, as little will in the one, as honesty in the other. S'foote ile into the country againe, learne to speake truth, drinke Ale, and conuerse with my fathers Tenants; here I heare nothing all day, but vpon my soule as I am a Gentleman, and an honest man.

AYMER
I vow and affirme, your Taylor must needs be an expert
Geometrician, he has the Longitude, Latitude, Altitude,
Profundity, euery Demension of your body, so exquisitely,
Here's a lace layd as directly, as if truth were a
Taylor.

PAGE
That were a miracle.

LILLADAM
With a haire breadth's errour, ther's a shoulder piece cut, and the base of a pickadille in puncto.

AYMER
You are right, Mounsieur his vestaments fit: as if they grew vpon him, or art had wrought 'em on the same loome, as nature fram'd his Lordship as if your Taylor were deepely read in Astrology, and had taken measure of your honourable body, with a Iacobs staffe, an Ephimerides.

TAYLOR
I am bound t'ee Gentlemen.

PAGE
You are deceiu'd, they'll be bound to you, you must remember to trust 'em none.

NOUALL JUNIOR
Nay, fayth, thou art a reasonable neat Artificer, giue the diuell his due.

PAGE
I, if hee would but cut the coate according to the cloth still.

NOUALL JUNIOR
I now want onely my misters approbation, who is indeed, the most polite punctuall Queene of dressing in all Burgundy. Pah, and makes all other young Ladies appeare, as if they came from boord last weeke out of the country, Is't not true, Liladam?

LILLADAM

True my Lord, as if any thing your Lordship could say, could be othewrise then true.

NOUALL JUNIOR
Nay, a my soule, 'tis so, what fouler obiect in the world, then to see a young faire, handsome beauty, vnhandsomely dighted and incongruently accoutred; or a hopefull Cheualier, vnmethodically appointed, in the externall ornaments of nature? For euen as the Index tels vs the contents of stories, and directs to the particular Chapters, euen so does the outward habit and superficiall order of garments (in man or woman) giue vs a tast of the spirit, and demonstratiuely poynt (as it were a manuall note from the margin) all the internall quality, and habiliment of the soule, and there cannot be a more euident, palpable, grosse manifestation of poore degenerate dunghilly blood, and breeding, then rude, vnpolish'd, disordered and slouenly outside.

PAGE
An admirable! lecture. Oh all you gallants, that hope to be saued by your cloathes, edify, edify.

AYMER
By the Lard, sweet Lard, thou deseru'st a pension
o' the State.

PAGE
O th' Taylors, two such Lords were able to spread
Taylors ore the face of a whole kingdome.

NOUALL JUNIOR
Pox a this glasse! it flatters, I could find in my heart
to breake it.

PAGE
O saue the glasse my Lord, and breake their heads,
they are the greater flatterers I assure you.

AYMER
Flatters, detracts, impayres, yet put it by,
Lest thou deare Lord (Narcissus-like) should doate
Vpon thyselfe, and dye; and rob the world
Of natures copy, that she workes forme by.

LILLADAM
Oh that I were the Infanta Queene of Europe,
Who (but thy selfe sweete Lord) shouldst marry me.

NOUALL JUNIOR
I marry? were there a Queene oth' world, not I.
Wedlocke? no padlocke, horselocke, I weare spurrs

[He capers.

To keepe it off my heeles; yet my Aymour,

Like a free wanton iennet i'th meddows,
I looke aboute, and neigh, take hedge and ditch,
Feede in my neighbours pastures, picke my choyce
Of all their faire-maind-mares: but married once,
A man is stak'd, or pown'd, and cannot graze
Beyond his owne hedge.

[Enter **PONTALIER**, and **MALOTIN**.

PONTALIER
I haue waited, sir,
Three hours to speake w'ee, and not take it well,
Such magpies are admitted, whilst I daunce
Attendance.

LILLADAM
Magpies? what d'ee take me for?

PONTALIER
A long thing with a most vnpromising face.

AYMER
I'll ne're aske him what he takes me for?

MALOTIN
Doe not, sir,
For hee'l goe neere to tell you.

PONTALIER
Art not thou
A Barber Surgeon?

BARBER
Yes sira why.

PONTALIER
My Lord is sorely troubled with two scabs.

LILLADAM
AYMER
Humph—

PONTALIER
I prethee cure him of 'em.

NOUALL JUNIOR
Pish: no more,
Thy gall sure's ouer throwne; these are my Councell,

And we were now in serious discourse.

PONTALIER
Of perfume and apparell, can you rise
And spend 5 houres in dressing talke, with these?

NOUALL JUNIOR
Thou 'idst haue me be a dog: vp, stretch and shake,
And ready for all day.

PONTALIER
Sir, would you be
More curious in preseruing of your honour.
Trim, 'twere more manly. I am come to wake
Your reputation, from this lethargy
You let it sleep in, to perswade, importune,
Nay, to prouoke you, sir, to call to account
This Collonell Romont, for the foule wrong
Which like a burthen, he hath layd on you,
And like a drunken porter, you sleepe vnder.
'Tis all the towne talkes, and beleeue, sir,
If your tough sense persist thus, you are vndone,
Vtterly lost, you will be scornd and baffled
By euery Lacquay; season now your youth,
With one braue thing, and it shall keep the odour
Euen to your death, beyond, and on your Tombe,
Sent like sweet oyles and Frankincense; sir, this life
Which once you sau'd, I ne're since counted mine,
I borrow'd it of you; and now will pay it;
I tender you the seruice of my sword
To beare your challenge, if you'll write, your fate:
Ile make mine owne: what ere betide you, I
That haue liu'd by you, by your side will dye.

NOUALL JUNIOR
Ha, ha, would'st ha' me challenge poore Romont?
Fight with close breeches, thou mayst think I dare not.
Doe not mistake me (cooze) I am very valiant,
But valour shall not make me such an Asse.
What vse is there of valour (now a dayes?)
'Tis sure, or to be kill'd, or to be hang'd.
Fight thou as thy minde moues thee, 'tis thy trade,
Thou hast nothing else to doe; fight with Romont?
No i'le not fight vnder a Lord.

PONTALIER
Farewell, sir,
I pitty you.

Such louing Lords walke their dead honours graues,
For no companions fit, but fooles and knaues.
Come Malotin.

[Exeunt **PONTALIER, MALOTIN**.

[Enter **ROMONT**.

LILLADAM
’Sfoot, Colbran, the low gyant.

AYMER
He has brought a battaile in his face, let’s goe.

PAGE
Colbran d’ee call him? hee’l make some of you smoake,
I beleeue.

ROMONT
By your leaue, sirs.

AYMER
Are you a Consort?

ROMONT
D’ee take mee
For a fidler? ya’re deceiu’d: Looke. Ile pay you.

[Kickes ’em.

PAGE
It seemes he knows you one, he bumfiddles you so.

LILLADAM
Was there euer so base a fellow?

AYMER
A rascall?

LILLADAM
A most vnciuill Groome?

AYMER
Offer to kicke a Gentleman, in a Noblemans chamber?
A pox of your manners.

LILLADAM
Let him alone, let him alone, thou shalt lose thy

arme, fellow: if we stirre against thee, hang vs.

PAGE
S'foote, I thinke they haue the better on him,
though they be kickd, they talke so.

LILLADAM
Let's leaue the mad Ape.

NOUALL JUNIOR
Gentlemen.

LILLADAM
Nay, my Lord, we will not offer to dishonour you
so much as to stay by you, since hee's alone.

NOUALL JUNIOR
Harke you.

AYMER
We doubt the cause, and will not disparage you, so
much as to take your Lordships quarrel in hand. Plague on
him, how he has crumpled our bands.

PAGE
Ile eene away with 'em, for this souldier beates
man, woman, and child.

[Exeunt. Manent **ROMONT**.

NOUALL JUNIOR
What meane you, sir? My people.

ROMONT
Your boye's gone.

[Lockes the doore.

And doore's lockt, yet for no hurt to you,
But priuacy: call vp your blood againe, sir,
Be not affraid, I do beseach you, sir,
(And therefore come) without, more circumstance
Tell me how farre the passages haue gone
'Twixt you and your faire Mistresse Beaumelle,
Tell me the truth, and by my hope of Heauen
It neuer shall goe further.

NOUALL JUNIOR

Tell you why sir?
Are you my confessor?

ROMONT
I will be your confounder, if you doe not.

[Drawes a pocket dag.

Stirre not, nor spend your voyce.

NOUALL JUNIOR
What will you doe?

ROMONT
Nothing but lyne your brayne-pan, sir, with lead,
If you not satisfie me suddenly,
I am desperate of my life, and command yours.

NOUALL JUNIOR
Hold, hold, ile speake. I vow to heauen and you,
Shee's yet vntouch't, more then her face and hands:
I cannot call her innocent; for I yeeld
On my sollicitous wrongs she consented
Where time and place met oportunity
To grant me all requests.

ROMONT
But may I build
On this assurance?

NOUALL JUNIOR
As vpon your fayth.

ROMONT
Write this, sir, nay you must.

[Drawes Inkehorne and paper.

NOUALL JUNIOR
Pox of this Gunne.

ROMONT
Withall, sir, you must sweare, and put your oath
Vnder your hand, (shake not) ne're to frequent
This Ladies company, nor euer send
Token, or message, or letter, to incline
This (too much prone already) yeelding Lady.

NOUALL JUNIOR
'Tis done, sir.

ROMONT
Let me see, this first is right,
And heere you wish a sudden death may light
Vpon your body, and hell take your soule,
If euer more you see her, but by chance,
Much lesse allure. Now, my Lord, your hand.

NOUALL JUNIOR
My hand to this?

ROMONT
Your heart else I assure you.

NOUALL JUNIOR
Nay, there 'tis.

ROMONT
So keepe this last article
Of your fayth giuen, and stead of threatnings, sir,
The seruice of my sword and life is yours:
But not a word of it, 'tis Fairies treasure;
Which but reueal'd, brings on the blabbers, ruine.
Vse your youth better, and this excellent forme
Heauen hath bestowed vpon you.
So good morrow to your Lordship.

NOUALL JUNIOR
Good diuell to your rogueship. No man's safe:
Ile haue a Cannon planted in my chamber,

[Exit.

Against such roaring roagues.

[Enter **BELLAPERT**.

BELLAPERT
My Lord away
The Coach stayes: now haue your wish, and iudge,
If I haue been forgetfull.

NOUALL JUNIOR
Ha?

BELLAPERT

D’ee stand
Humming and hawing now?

[Exit.

NOUALL JUNIOR
Sweet wench, I come.
Hence feare,
I swore, that’s all one, my next oath ’ile keepe
That I did meane to breake, and then ’tis quit.
No paine is due to louers periury.
If loue himselfe laugh at it, so will I.

[Exit **NOUALL JUNIOR**.

SCENE II

An outer Room in Aymer’s House

Enter **CHARALOIS, BAUMONT**.

BAUMONT
I grieue for the distaste, though I haue manners,
Not to inquire the cause, falne out betweene
Your Lordship and Romont.

CHARALOIS
I loue a friend,
So long as he continues in the bounds
Prescrib’d by friendship, but when he vsurpes
Too farre on what is proper to my selfe,
And puts the habit of a Gouernor on,
I must and will preserue my liberty.
But speake of something, else this is a theame
I take no pleasure in: what’s this Aymeire,
Whose voyce for Song, and excellent knowledge in
The chiefest parts of Musique, you bestow
Such prayses on?

BAUMONT
He is a Gentleman,
(For so his quality speakes him) well receiu’d
Among our greatest Gallants; but yet holds
His maine dependance from the young Lord Nouall:
Some tricks and crotchets he has in his head,
As all Musicians haue, and more of him

I dare not author: but when you haue heard him,
I may presume, your Lordship so will like him,
That you'l hereafter be a friend to Musique.

CHARALOIS
I neuer was an enemy to't, Baumont,
Nor yet doe I subscribe to the opinion
Of those old Captaines, that thought nothing musicall,
But cries of yeelding enemies, neighing of horses,
Clashing of armour, lowd shouts, drums, and trumpets:
Nor on the other side in fauour of it,
Affirme the world was made by musicall discord,
Or that the happinesse of our life consists
In a well varied note vpon the Lute:
I loue it to the worth of it, and no further.
But let vs see this wonder.

BAUMONT
He preuents
My calling of him.

AYMER
Let the Coach be brought

[Enter **AYMER**.

To the backe gate, and serue the banquet vp:
My good Lord Charalois, I thinke my house
Much honor'd in your presence.

CHARALOIS
To haue meanes
To know you better, sir, has brought me hither
A willing visitant, and you'l crowne my welcome
In making me a witnesse to your skill,
Which crediting from others I admire.

AYMER
Had I beene one houre sooner made acquainted
With your intent my Lord, you should haue found me
Better prouided: now such as it is,
Pray you grace with your acceptance.

BAUMONT
You are modest.
Begin the last new ayre.

CHARALOIS

Shall we not see them?

AYMER
This little distance from the instruments
Will to your eares conuey the harmony
With more delight.

CHARALOIS
Ile not consent.

AYMER
Y'are tedious,
By this meanes shall I with one banquet please
Two companies, those within and these Guls heere.

[Song aboue.

[CITTIZENS SONG OF THE COURTIER.

Courtier, if thou needs wilt wiue,
From this lesson learne to thriue.
If thou match a Lady, that
Passes thee in birth and state,
Let her curious garments be
Twice aboue thine owne degree;
This will draw great eyes vpon her,
Get her seruants and thee honour.

BEAUMELLE [within—ha, ha, ha.

CHARALOIS
How's this? It is my Ladies laugh! most certaine
When I first pleas'd her, in this merry language,
She gaue me thanks.

BAUMONT
How like you this?

CHARALOIS
'Tis rare,
Yet I may be deceiu'd, and should be sorry
Vpon vncertaine suppositions, rashly
To write my selfe in the blacke list of those
I haue declaym'd against, and to Romont.

AYMER
I would he were well of—perhaps your Lordship
Likes not these sad tunes, I haue a new Song

Set to a lighter note, may please you better;
Tis cal'd The happy husband.

CHARALOIS
Pray sing it.

[Song below.

[COURTIERS SONG OF THE CITIZEN.

Poore Citizen, if thou wilt be
A happy husband, learne of me;
To set thy wife first in thy shop,
A faire wife, a kinde wife, a sweet wife, sets a poore man vp.
What though thy shelues be ne're so bare:
A woman still is currant ware:
Each man will cheapen, foe, and friend,
But whilst thou art at tother end,
What ere thou seest, or what dost heare,
Foole, haue no eye to, nor an eare;
And after supper for her sake,
When thou hast fed, snort, though thou wake:
What though the Gallants call thee mome?
Yet with thy lanthorne light her home:
Then looke into the town and tell,
If no such Tradesmen there doe dwell.

[At the end of the Song, **BEAUMELLE** within.

BEAUMELLE
Ha, ha, 'tis such a groome.

CHARALOIS
Doe I heare this,
And yet stand doubtfull?

[Exit **CHARALOIS**.

AYMER
Stay him I am vndone,
And they discouered.

BAUMONT
Whats the matter?

AYMER
Ah!
That women, when they are well pleas'd, cannot hold,

But must laugh out.

[Enter **NOUALL JUNIOR, CHARALOIS, BEAUMELLE, BELLAPERT**.

NOUALL JUNIOR
Helpe, saue me, murrher, murther.

BEAUMELLE
Vndone foreuer.

CHARALOIS
Oh, my heart!
Hold yet a little—doe not hope to scape
By flight, it is impossible: though I might
On all aduantage take thy life, and iustly;
This sword, my fathers sword, that nere was drawne,
But to a noble purpose, shall not now
Doe th' office of a hangman, I reserue it
To right mine honour, not for a reuenge
So poore, that though with thee, it should cut off
Thy family, with all that are allyed
To thee in lust, or basenesse, 'twere still short of
All termes of satisfaction. Draw.

NOUALL JUNIOR
I dare not,
I haue already done you too much wrong,
To fight in such a cause.

CHARALOIS
Why, darest thou neyther
Be honest, coward, nor yet valiant, knaue?
In such a cause come doe not shame thy selfe:
Such whose bloods wrongs, or wrong done to themselues
Could neuer heate, are yet in the defence
Of their whores, daring looke on her againe.
You thought her worth the hazard of your soule,
And yet stand doubtfull in her quarrell, to
Venture your body.

BAUMONT
No, he feares his cloaths,
More then his flesh

CHARALOIS
Keepe from me, garde thy life,
Or as thou hast liu'd like a goate, thou shalt
Dye like a sheepe.

NOUALL JUNIOR
Since ther's no remedy

[They fight, **NOUALL JUNIOR** is slaine.

Despaire of safety now in me proue courage.

CHARALOIS
How soone weak wrong's or'throwne! lend me your hand,
Beare this to the Caroach—come, you haue taught me
To say you must and shall: I wrong you not,
Y'are but to keepe him company you loue.
Is't done? 'tis well. Raise officers, and take care,
All you can apprehend within the house
May be forth comming. Do I appeare much mou'd?

BAUMONT
No, sir.

CHARALOIS
My griefes are now, Thus to be borne.
Hereafter ile finde time and place to mourne.

[Exeunt.

SCENE III

A Street

Enter **ROMONT, PONTALIER**.

PONTALIER
I was bound to seeke you, sir.

ROMONT
And had you found me
In any place, but in the streete, I should
Haue done,—not talk'd to you. Are you the Captaine?
The hopefull Pontalier? whom I haue seene
Doe in the field such seruice, as then made you
Their enuy that commanded, here at home
To play the parasite to a gilded knaue,
And it may be the Pander.

PONTALIER

Without this
I come to call you to account, for what
Is past already. I by your example
Of thankfulnesse to the dead Generall
By whom you were rais'd, haue practis'd to be so
To my good Lord Nouall, by whom I liue;
Whose least disgrace that is, or may be offred,
With all the hazzard of my life and fortunes,
I will make good on you, or any man,
That has a hand in't; and since you allowe me
A Gentleman and a souldier, there's no doubt
You will except against me. You shall meete
With a faire enemy, you vnderstand
The right I looke for, and must haue.

ROMONT
I doe,
And with the next dayes sunne you shall heare from me.

[Exeunt.

SCENE IV

A Room in Charalois' House

Enter **CHARALOIS** with a casket, **BEAUMELLE, BAUMONT**.

CHARALOIS
Pray beare this to my father, at his leasure
He may peruse it: but with your best language
Intreat his instant presence: you haue sworne
Not to reueale what I haue done.

BAUMONT
Nor will I—
But—

CHARALOIS
Doubt me not, by Heauen, I will doe nothing
But what may stand with honour: Pray you leaue me
To my owne thoughts. If this be to me, rise;
I am not worthy the looking on, but onely
To feed contempt and scorne, and that from you
Who with the losse of your faire name haue caus'd it,
Were too much cruelty.

BEAUMELLE
I dare not moue you
To heare me speake. I know my fault is farre
Beyond qualification, or excuse,
That 'tis not fit for me to hope, or you
To thinke of mercy; onely I presume
To intreate, you would be pleas'd to looke vpon
My sorrow for it, and beleeue, these teares
Are the true children of my griefe and not
A womans cunning.

CHARALOIS
Can you Beaumelle,
Hauing deceiued so great a trust as mine,
Though I were all credulity, hope againe
To get beleefe? no, no, if you looke on me
With pity or dare practise any meanes
To make my sufferings lesse, or giue iust cause
To all the world, to thinke what I must doe
Was cal'd vpon by you, vse other waies,
Deny what I haue seene, or iustifie
What you haue done, and as you desperately
Made shipwracke of your fayth to be a whore,
Vse th' armes of such a one, and such defence,
And multiply the sinne, with impudence,
Stand boldly vp, and tell me to my teeth,
You haue done but what's warranted,
By great examples, in all places, where
Women inhabit, vrge your owne deserts,
Or want of me in merit; tell me how,
Your dowre from the lowe gulfe of pouerty,
Weighed vp my fortunes, to what now they are:
That I was purchas'd by your choyse and practise
To shelter you from shame: that you might sinne
As boldly as securely, that poore men
Are married to those wiues that bring them wealth,
One day their husbands, but obseruers euer:
That when by this prou'd vsage you haue blowne
The fire of my iust vengeance to the height,
I then may kill you: and yet say 'twas done
In heate of blood, and after die my selfe,
To witnesse my repentance.

BEAUMELLE
O my fate,
That neuer would consent that I should see,
How worthy thou wert both of loue and duty
Before I lost you; and my misery made

The glasse, in which I now behold your vertue:
While I was good, I was a part of you,
And of two, by the vertuous harmony
Of our faire minds, made one; but since I wandred
In the forbidden Labyrinth of lust,
What was inseparable, is by me diuided.
With iustice therefore you may cut me off,
And from your memory, wash the remembrance
That ere I was like to some vicious purpose
Within your better iudgement, you repent of
And study to forget.

CHARALOIS
O Beaumelle,
That you can speake so well, and doe so ill!
But you had been too great a blessing, if
You had continued chast: see how you force me
To this, because my honour will not yeeld
That I againe should loue you.

BEAUMELLE
In this life
It is not fit you should: yet you shall finde,
Though I was bold enough to be a strumpet,
I dare not yet liue one: let those fam'd matrones
That are canoniz'd worthy of our sex,
Transcend me in their sanctity of life,
I yet will equall them in dying nobly,
Ambitious of no honour after life,
But that when I am dead, you will forgiue me.

CHARALOIS
How pity steales vpon me! should I heare her
But ten words more, I were lost—one knocks, go in.

[Knock within. Exit **BEAUMELLE**. Enter **ROCHFORT**.

That to be mercifull should be a sinne.
O, sir, most welcome. Let me take your cloake,
I must not be denyed—here are your robes,
As you loue iustice once more put them on:
There is a cause to be determind of
That doe's require such an integrity,
As you haue euer vs'd—ile put you to
The tryall of your constancy, and goodnesse:
And looke that you that haue beene Eagle-eyd
In other mens affaires, proue not a Mole
In what concernes your selfe. Take you your seate:

I will be for you presently.

[Exit.

ROCHFORT
Angels guard me,
To what strange Tragedy does this destruction
Serue for a Prologue?

[Enter **CHARALOIS** with **NOUALL JUNIOR'S** body. **BEAUMELLE, BAUMONT**.

CHARALOIS
So, set it downe before
The Iudgement seate, and stand you at the bar:
For me? I am the accuser.

ROCHFORT
Nouall slayne,
And Beaumelle my daughter in the place
Of one to be arraign'd.

CHARALOIS
O, are you touch'd?
I finde that I must take another course,
Feare nothing. I will onely blind your eyes,
For Iustice should do so, when 'tis to meete
An obiect that may sway her equall doome
From what it should be aim'd at.—Good my Lord,
A day of hearing.

ROCHFORT
It is granted, speake—
You shall haue iustice.

CHARALOIS
I then here accuse,
Most equall Iudge, the prisoner your faire Daughter,
For whom I owed so much to you: your daughter,
So worthy in her owne parts: and that worth
Set forth by yours, to whose so rare perfections,
Truth witnesse with me, in the place of seruice
I almost pay'd Idolatrous sacrifice
To be a false advltresse.

ROCHFORT
With whom?

CHARALOIS

With this Nouall here dead.

ROCHFORT
Be wel aduis'd
And ere you say adultresse againe,
Her fame depending on it, be most sure
That she is one.

CHARALOIS
I tooke them in the act.
I know no proofe beyond it.

ROCHFORT
O my heart.

CHARALOIS
A Iudge should feele no passions.

ROCHFORT
Yet remember
He is a man, and cannot put off nature.
What answere makes the prisoner?

BEAUMELLE
I confesse
The fact I am charg'd with, and yeeld my selfe
Most miserably guilty.

ROCHFORT
Heauen take mercy
Vpon your soule then: it must leaue your body.
Now free mine eyes, I dare vnmou'd looke on her,
And fortifie my sentence, with strong reasons.
Since that the politique law prouides that seruants,
To whose care we commit our goods shall die,
If they abuse our trust: what can you looke for,
To whose charge this most hopefull Lord gaue vp
All he receiu'd from his braue Ancestors,
Or he could leaue to his posterity?
His Honour, wicked woman, in whose safety
All his lifes ioyes, and comforts were locked vp,
With thy lust, a theefe hath now stolne from him,
And therefore—

CHARALOIS
Stay, iust Iudge, may not what's lost
By her owne fault, (for I am charitable,
And charge her not with many) be forgotten

In her faire life hereafter?

ROCHFORT
Neuer, Sir.
The wrong that's done to the chaste married bed,
Repentant teares can neuer expiate,
And be assured, to pardon such a sinne,
Is an offence as great as to commit it.

CHARALOIS
I may not then forgiue her.

ROCHFORT
Nor she hope it.
Nor can she wish to liue no sunne shall rise,
But ere it set, shall shew her vgly lust
In a new shape, and euery on more horrid:
Nay, euen those prayers, which with such humble feruor
She seemes to send vp yonder, are beate backe,
And all suites, which her penitance can proffer,
As soone as made, are with contempt throwne
Off all the courts of mercy.

[He kills her.

CHARALOIS
Let her die then.
Better prepar'd I am. Sure I could not take her,
Nor she accuse her father, as a Iudge
Partiall against her.

BEAUMELLE
I approue his sentence,
And kisse the executioner; my lust
Is now run from me in that blood; in which
It was begot and nourished.

ROCHFORT
Is she dead then?

CHARALOIS
Yes, sir, this is her heart blood, is it not?
I thinke it be.

ROCHFORT
And you haue kild here?

CHARALOIS

True,
And did it by your doome

ROCHFORT
But I pronounc'd it
As a Iudge onely, and friend to iustice,
And zealous in defence of your wrong'd honour,
Broke all the tyes of nature: and cast off
The loue and soft affection of a father.
I in your cause, put on a Scarlet robe
Of red died cruelty, but in returne,
You haue aduanc'd for me no flag of mercy:
I look'd on you, as a wrong'd husband, but
You clos'd your eyes against me, as a father.
O Beaumelle, my daughter.

CHARALOIS
This is madnesse.

ROCHFORT
Keepe from me—could not one good thought rise vp,
To tell you that she was my ages comfort,
Begot by a weake man, and borne a woman,
And could not therefore, but partake of frailety?
Or wherefore did not thankfulnesse step forth,
To vrge my many merits, which I may
Obiect vnto you, since you proue vngratefull,
Flinty-hearted Charalois?

CHARALOIS
Nature does preuaile
Aboue your vertue.

ROCHFORT
No! it giues me eyes,
To pierce the heart of designe against me.
I finde it now, it was my state was aym'd at,
A nobler match was fought for, and the houres
I liu'd, grew teadious to you: my compassion
Towards you hath rendred me most miserable,
And foolish charity vndone my selfe:
But ther's a Heauen aboue, from whose iust wreake
No mists of policy can hide offendors.

[Enter **NOUALL SENIOR** with **OFFICERS**.

NOUALL SENIOR
Force ope the doors—O monster, caniball,

Lay hold on him, my sonne, my sonne.—O Rochfort,
'Twas you gaue liberty to this bloody wolfe
To worry all our comforts,—But this is
No time to quarrell; now giue your assistance
For the reuenge.

ROCHFORT
Call it a fitter name—
Iustice for innocent blood.

CHARALOIS
Though all conspire
Against that life which I am weary of,
A little longer yet ile striue to keepe it,
To shew in spite of malice, and their lawes,
His plea must speed that hath an honest cause.

[Exeunt

ACTUS QUINTUS

SCENE I

A Street

Enter **LILLADAM**, **TAYLOR**, **OFFICERS**.

LILLADAM
Why 'tis both most vnconscionable, and vntimely
T'arrest a gallant for his cloaths, before
He has worne them out: besides you sayd you ask'd
My name in my Lords bond but for me onely,
And now you'l lay me vp for't. Do not thinke
The taking measure of a customer
By a brace of varlets, though I rather wait
Neuer so patiently, will proue a fashion
Which any Courtier or Innes of court man
Would follow willingly.

TAYLOR
There I beleeue you.
But sir, I must haue present moneys, or
Assurance to secure me, when I shall.—
Or I will see to your comming forth.

LILLADAM

Plague on't,
You haue prouided for my enterance in:
That comming forth you talke of, concernes me.
What shall I doe? you haue done me a disgrace
In the arrest, but more in giuing cause
To all the street, to thinke I cannot stand
Without these two supporters for my armes:
Pray you let them loose me: for their satisfaction
I will not run away.

TAYLOR
For theirs you will not,
But for your owne you would; looke to them fellows.

LILLADAM
Why doe you call them fellows? doe not wrong
Your reputation so, as you are meerely
A Taylor, faythfull, apt to beleeue in Gallants
You are a companion at a ten crowne supper
For cloth of bodkin, and may with one Larke
Eate vp three manchets, and no man obserue you,
Or call your trade in question for't. But when
You study your debt-booke, and hold correspondence
With officers of the hanger, and leaue swordmen,
The learned conclude, the Taylor and Sergeant
In the expression of a knaue are these
To be Synonima. Looke therefore to it,
And let vs part in peace, I would be loth
You should vndoe your selfe.

TAYLOR
To let you goe

[Enter **NOUALL SENIOR**, and **PONTALIER**.

Were the next way.
But see! heeres your old Lord,
Let him but giue his worde I shall be paide,
And you are free.

LILLADAM
S'lid, I will put him to't:
I can be but denied: or what say you?
His Lordship owing me three times your debt,
If you arrest him at my suite, and let me
Goe run before to see the action entred.
'Twould be a witty iest.

TAYLOR
I must haue ernest:
I cannot pay my debts so.

PONTALIER
Can your Lordship
Imagine, while I liue and weare a sword,
Your sonnes death shall be reueng'd?

NOUALL SENIOR
I know not
One reason why you should not doe like others:
I am sure, of all the herd that fed vpon him,
I cannot see in any, now hee's gone,
In pitty or in thankfulnesse one true signe
Of sorrow for him.

PONTALIER
All his bounties yet
Fell not in such vnthankfull ground: 'tis true
He had weakenesses, but such as few are free from,
And though none sooth'd them lesse then I: for now
To say that I foresaw the dangers that
Would rise from cherishing them, were but vntimely.
I yet could wish the iustice that you seeke for
In the reuenge, had been trusted to me,
And not the vncertaine issue of the lawes:
'Tas rob'd me of a noble testimony
Of what I durst doe for him: but howeuer,
My forfait life redeem'd by him though dead,
Shall doe him seruice.

NOUALL SENIOR
As farre as my griefe
Will giue me leaue, I thanke you.

LILLADAM
Oh my Lord,
Oh my good Lord, deliuer me from these furies.

PONTALIER
Arrested? This is one of them whose base
And obiect flattery helpt to digge his graue:
He is not worth your pitty, nor my anger.
Goe to the basket and repent.

NOUALL SENIOR
Away

I onely know now to hate thee deadly:
I will doe nothing for thee.

LILLADAM
Nor you, Captaine.

PONTALIER
No, to your trade againe, put off this case,
It may be the discouering what you were,
When your vnfortunate master tooke you vp,
May moue compassion in your creditor.
Confesse the truth.

[Exit **NOUALL SENIOR, PONTALIER**.

LILLADAM
And now I thinke on't better,
I will, brother, your hand, your hand, sweet brother.
I am of your sect, and my gallantry but a dreame,
Out of which these two fearefull apparitions
Against my will haue wak'd me. This rich sword
Grew suddenly out of a taylors bodkin;
These hangers from my vailes and fees in Hell:
And where as now this beauer sits, full often
A thrifty cape compos'd of broad cloth lifts,
Nere kin vnto the cushion where I sate.
Crosse-leg'd, and yet vngartred, hath beene seene,
Our breakefasts famous for the buttred loaues,
I haue with ioy bin oft acquainted with,
And therefore vse a conscience, though it be
Forbidden in our hall towards other men,
To me that as I haue beene, will againe
Be of the brotherhood.

OFFICER
I know him now:
He was a prentice to Le Robe at Orleance.

LILLADAM
And from thence brought by my young Lord, now dead,
Vnto Dijon, and with him till this houre
Hath bin receiu'd here for a compleate Mounsieur.
Nor wonder at it: for but tythe our gallants,
Euen those of the first ranke, and you will finde
In euery ten, one: peraduenture two,
That smell ranke of the dancing schoole, or fiddle,
The pantofle or pressing yron: but hereafter
Weele talke of this. I will surrender vp

My suites againe: there cannot be much losse,
'Tis but the turning of the lace, with ones
Additions more you know of, and what wants
I will worke out.

TAYLOR
Then here our quarrell ends.
The gallant is turn'd Taylor, and all friends.

[Exeunt.

SCENE II

The Court of Justice

Enter **ROMONT, BAUMONT**.

ROMONT
You haue them ready.

BAUMONT
Yes, and they will speake
Their knowledg in this cause, when thou thinkst fit
To haue them cal'd vpon.

ROMONT
'Tis well, and something
I can adde to their euidence, to proue
This braue reuenge, which they would haue cal'd murther,
A noble Iustice.

BAUMONT
In this you expresse
(The breach by my Lords want of you, new made vp)
A faythfull friend.

ROMONT
That friendship's rays'd on sand,
Which euery sudden gust of discontent,
Or flowing of our passions can change,
As if it nere had bin: but doe you know
Who are to sit on him?

BAUMONT
Mounsieur Du Croy
Assisted by Charmi.

ROMONT
The Aduocate
That pleaded for the Marshalls funerall,
And was checkt for it by Nouall.

BAUMONT
The same

ROMONT
How fortunes that?

BAUMONT
Why, sir, my Lord Nouall
Being the accuser, cannot be the Iudge,
Nor would grieue Rochfort, but Lord Charaloys
(Howeuer he might wrong him by his power,)
Should haue an equall hearing.

ROMONT
By my hopes
Of Charaloys acquitall, I lament
That reuerent old mans fortune.

BAUMONT
Had you seene him,
As to my griefe I haue now promis'd patience,
And ere it was beleeu'd, though spake by him
That neuer brake his word, inrag'd againe
So far as to make warre vpon those heires
Which not a barbarous Sythian durst presume
To touch, but with a superstitious feare,
As something sacred, and then curse his daughter,
But with more frequent violence himselfe,
As if he had bin guilty of her fault,
By being incredulous of your report,
You would not onely iudge him worrhy pitty,
But suffer with him.

[Enter **CHARALOIS**, with **OFFICERS**.

But heere comes the prisoner,
I dare not stay to doe my duty to him,
Yet rest assur'd, all possible meanes in me
To doe him seruice, keepes you company.

[Exit **BAUMONT**.

ROMONT
It is not doubted.

CHARALOIS
Why, yet as I came hither,
The people apt to mocke calamity,
And tread on the oppress'd, made no hornes at me,
Though they are too familiar: I deserue them.
And knowing what blood my sword hath drunke
In wreake of that disgrace, they yet forbare
To shake their heads, or to reuile me for
A murtherer, they rather all put on
(As for great losses the old Romans vs'd)
A generall face of sorrow, waighted on
By a sad murmur breaking through their silence,
And no eye but was readier with a teare
To witnesse 'twas shed for me, then I could
Discerne a face made vp with scorne against me.
Why should I then, though for vnusuall wrongs,
I chose vnusuall meanes to right those wrongs,
Condemne my selfe, as over-partiall
In my owne cause Romont?

ROMONT
Best friend, well met,

By my heart's loue to you, and ioyne to that,
My thankfulness that still liues to the dead,
I looke upon you now with more true ioy,
Than when I saw you married.

CHARALOIS
You have reason
To give you warrant for't; my falling off
From such a friendship with the scorne that answered
Your too propheticke counsell, may well moue you
To thinke your meeting me going to my death,
A fit encounter for that hate which iustly
I have deseru'd from you.

ROMONT
Shall I still then
Speake truth, and be ill vnderstood?

CHARALOIS
You are not.
I am conscious, I haue wrong'd you, and allow me
Only a morall man to looke on you,

Whom foolishly I haue abus'd and iniur'd,
Must of necessity be more terrible to me,
Than any death the Iudges can pronounce
From the tribunall which I am to plead at.

ROMONT
Passion transports you.

CHARALOIS
For what I haue done
To my false Lady, or Nouall, I can
Giue some apparent cause: but touching you,
In my defence, childlike, I can say nothing,
But I am sorry for't, a poore satisfaction:
And yet mistake me not: for it is more
Then I will speake, to haue my pardon sign'd
For all I stand accus'd of.

ROMONT
You much weaken
The strength of your good cause. Should you but thinke
A man for doing well could entertaine
A pardon, were it offred, you haue giuen
To blinde and slow-pac'd iustice, wings, and eyes
To see and ouertake impieties,
Which from a cold proceeding had receiu'd
Indulgence or protection.

CHARALOIS
Thinke you so?

ROMONT
Vpon my soule nor should the blood you chalenge
And took to cure your honour, breed more scruple
In your soft conscience, then if your sword
Had bin sheath'd in a Tygre, or she Beare,
That in their bowels would haue made your tombe
To iniure innocence is more then murther:
But when inhumane lusts transforme vs, then
Like beasts we are to suffer, not like men
To be lamented. Nor did Charalois euer
Performe an act so worthy the applause
Of a full theater of perfect men,
As he hath done in this: the glory got
By ouerthrowing outward enemies,
Since strength and fortune are maine sharers in it,
We cannot but by pieces call our owne:
But when we conquer our intestine foes,

Our passions breed within vs, and of those
The most rebellious tyrant powerfull loue,
Our reason suffering vs to like no longer
Then the faire obiect being good deserues it,
That's a true victory, which, were great men
Ambitious to atchieue, by your example
Setting no price vpon the breach of fayth,
But losse of life, 'twould fright adultery
Out of their families, and make lust appeare
As lothsome to vs in the first consent,
As when 'tis wayted on by punishment.

CHARALOIS
You haue confirm'd me. Who would loue a woman
That might inioy in such a man, a friend?
You haue made me know the iustice of my cause,
And mark't me out the way, how to defend it.

ROMONT
Continue to that resolution constant,
And you shall, in contempt of their worst malice,
Come off with honour. Heere they come.

CHARALOIS
I am ready.

SCENE III

Enter **Du CROY, CHARMI, ROCHFORT, NOUALL SENIOR, PONTALIER, BAUMONT**.

NOUALL SENIOR
See, equall Iudges, with what confidence
The cruel murtherer stands, as if he would
Outface the Court and Iustice!

ROCHFORT
But looke on him.
And you shall find, for still methinks I doe,
Though guilt hath dide him black, something good in him,
That may perhaps worke with a wiser man
Then I haue beene, againe to set him free
And giue him all he has.

CHARMI
This is not well.
I would you had liu'd so, my Lord that I,

Might rather haue continu'd your poore seruant,
Then sit here as your Iudge.

Du CROY
I am sorry for you.

ROCHFORT
In no act of my life I haue deseru'd
This iniury from the court, that any heere
Should thus vnciuilly vsurpe on what
Is proper to me only.

Du CROY
What distaste
Receiues my Lord?

ROCHFORT
You say you are sorry for him:
A griefe in which I must not haue a partner:
'Tis I alone am sorry, that I rays'd
The building of my life for seuenty yeeres
Vpon so sure a ground, that all the vices
Practis'd to ruine man, though brought against me,
Could neuer vndermine, and no way left
To send these gray haires to the graue with sorrow.
Vertue that was my patronesse betrayd me:
For entring, nay, possessing this young man,
It lent him such a powerfull Maiesty
To grace what ere he vndertooke, that freely
I gaue myselfe vp with my liberty,
To be at his disposing; had his person
Louely I must confesse, or far fain'd valour,
Or any other seeming good, that yet
Holds a neere neyghbour-hood, with ill wrought on me,
I might haue borne it better: but when goodnesse
And piety it selfe in her best figure
Were brib'd to by destruction, can you blame me,
Though I forget to suffer like a man,
Or rather act a woman?

BAUMONT
Good my Lord.

NOUALL SENIOR
You hinder our proceeding.

CHARMI
And forget

The parts of an accuser.

BAUMONT
Pray you remember
To vse the temper which to me you promis'd.

ROCHFORT
Angels themselues must breake Baumont, that promise
Beyond the strength and patience of Angels.
But I haue done, my good Lord, pardon me
A weake old man, and pray adde to that
A miserable father, yet be carefull
That your compassion of my age, nor his,
Moue you to anything, that may dis-become
The place on which you sit.

CHARMI
Read the Inditement.

CHARALOIS
It shall be needelesse, I my selfe, my Lords,
Will be my owne accuser, and confesse
All they can charge me with, or will I spare
To aggrauate that guilt with circumstance
They seeke to loade me with: onely I pray,
That as for them you will vouchsafe me hearing:
I may not be, denide it for my selfe,
When I shall vrge by what vnanswerable reasons
I was compel'd to what I did, which yet
Till you haue taught me better, I repent not.

ROCHFORT
The motion honest.

CHARMI
And 'tis freely granted.

CHARALOIS
Then I confesse my Lords, that I stood bound,
When with my friends, euen hope it selfe had left me
To this mans charity for my liberty,
Nor did his bounty end there, but began:
For after my enlargement, cherishing
The good he did, he made me master of
His onely daughter, and his whole estate:
Great ties of thankfulnesse I must acknowledge,
Could any one freed by you, presse this further
But yet consider, my most honourd Lords,

If to receiue a fauour, make a seruant,
And benefits are bonds to tie the taker
To the imperious will of him that giues,
Ther's none but slaues will receiue courtesie,
Since they must fetter vs to our dishonours.
Can it be cal'd magnificence in a Prince,
To powre downe riches, with a liberall hand,
Vpon a poore mans wants, if that must bind him
To play the soothing parasite to his vices?
Or any man, because he sau'd my hand,
Presume my head and heart are at his seruice?
Or did I stand ingag'd to buy my freedome
(When my captiuity was honourable)
By making my selfe here and fame hereafter,
Bondslaues to mens scorne and calumnious tongues?
Had his faire daughters mind bin like her feature,
Or for some little blemish I had sought
For my content elsewhere, wasting on others
My body and her dowry; my forhead then
Deseru'd the brand of base ingratitude:
But if obsequious vsage, and faire warning
To keepe her worth my loue, could preserue her
From being a whore, and yet no cunning one,
So to offend, and yet the fault kept from me?
What should I doe? let any freeborne spirit
Determine truly, if that thankfulnesse,
Choise forme with the whole world giuen for a dowry,
Could strengthen so an honest man with patience,
As with a willing necke to vndergoe
The insupportable yoake of slaue or wittoll.

CHARMI
What proofe haue you she did play false, besides
your oath?

CHARALOIS
Her owne confession to her father.
I aske him for a witnesse.

ROCHFORT
'Tis most true.
I would not willingly blend my last words
With an vntruth.

CHARALOIS
And then to cleere my selfe,
That his great wealth was not the marke I shot at,
But that I held it, when faire Beaumelle

Fell from her vertue, like the fatall gold
Which Brennus tooke from Delphos, whose possession
Brought with it ruine to himselfe and Army.
Heer's one in Court, Baumont, by whom I sent
All graunts and writings backe, which made it mine,
Before his daughter dy'd by his owne sentence,
As freely as vnask'd he gaue it to me.

BAUMONT
They are here to be seene.

CHARMI
Open the casket.
Peruse that deed of gift.

ROMONT
Halfe of the danger
Already is discharg'd: the other part
As brauely, and you are not onely free,
But crownd with praise for euer.

Du CROY
'Tis apparent.

CHARMI
Your state, my Lord, againe is yours.

ROCHFORT
Not mine,
I am not of the world, if it can prosper,
(And being iustly got, Ile not examine
Why it should be so fatall) doe you bestow it
On pious vses. Ile goe seeke a graue.
And yet for proofe, I die in peace, your pardon
I aske, and as you grant it me, may Heauen
Your conscience, and these Iudges free you from
What you are charg'd with. So farewell for euer.—

[Exit **ROCHFORT**.

NOUALL SENIOR
Ile be mine owne guide. Passion, nor example
Shall be my leaders. I haue lost a sonne,
A sonne, graue Iudges, I require his blood
From his accursed homicide.

CHARMI
What reply you

In your defence for this?

CHARALOIS
I but attended
Your Lordships pleasure. For the fact, as of
The former, I confesse it, but with what
Base wrongs I was vnwillingly drawne to it,
To my few wordes there are some other proofes
To witnesse this for truth, when I was married:
For there I must begin. The slayne Nouall
Was to my wife, in way of our French courtship,
A most deuoted seruant, but yet aym'd at
Nothing but meanes to quench his wanton heate,
His heart being neuer warm'd by lawfull fires
As mine was (Lords:) and though on these presumptions,
Ioyn'd to the hate betweene his house and mine,
I might with opportunity and ease
Haue found a way for my reuenge, I did not;
But still he had the freedome as before
When all was mine, and told that he abus'd it
With some vnseemely licence, by my friend
My appou'd friend Romont, I gaue no credit
To the reporter, but reprou'd him for it
As one vncourtly and malicious to him.
What could I more, my Lords? yet after this
He did continue in his first pursute
Hoter then euer, and at length obtaind it;
But how it came to my most certaine knowledge,
For the dignity of the court and my owne honour
I dare not say.

NOUALL SENIOR
If all may be beleeu'd
A passionate prisoner speakes, who is so foolish
That durst be wicked, that will appeare guilty?
No, my graue Lords: in his Impunity
But giue example vnto iealous men
To cut the throats they hate, and they will neuer
Want matter or pretence for their bad ends.

CHARMI
You must find other proofes to strengthen these
But more presumptions.

Du CROY
Or we shall hardly
Allow your innocence.

CHARALOIS
All your attempts
Shall fall on me, like brittle shafts on armour,
That breake themselues; or like waues against a rocke,
That leaue no signe of their ridiculous fury
But foame and splinters, my innocence like these
Shall stand triumphant, and your malice serue
But for a trumpet; to proclaime my conquest
Nor shall you, though you doe the worst fate can,
How ere condemne, affright an honest man.

ROMONT
May it please the Court, I may be heard.

NOUALL SENIOR
You come not
To raile againe? but doe, you shall not finde,
Another Rochfort.

ROMONT
In Nouall I cannot.
But I come furnished with what will stop
The mouth of his conspiracy against the life
Of innocent Charaloys. Doe you know this Character?

NOUALL SENIOR
Yes, 'tis my sonnes.

ROMONT
May it please your Lordships, reade it,
And you shall finde there, with what vehemency
He did sollicite Beaumelle, how he had got
A promise from her to inioy his wishes,
How after he abiur'd her company,
And yet, but that 'tis fit I spare the dead,
Like a damnd villaine, assoone as recorded,
He brake that oath, to make this manifest
Produce his bands and hers.

[Enter **AYMER, FLORIMELL, BELLAPERT**.

CHARMI
Haue they tooke their oathes?

ROMONT
They haue; and rather then indure the racke,
Confesse the time, the meeting, nay the act;
What would you more? onely this matron made

A free discouery to a good end;
And therefore I sue to the Court, she may not
Be plac'd in the blacke list of the delinquents.

PONTALIER
I see by this, Nouals reuenge needs me,
And I shall doe.

CHARMI
'Tis euident.

NOUALL SENIOR
That I
Till now was neuer wretched, here's no place
To curse him or my stars.

[Exit **NOUALL SENIOR**.

CHARMI
Lord Charalois,
The iniurie: you haue sustain'd, appeare
So worthy of the mercy of the Court,
That notwithstanding you haue gone beyond
The letter of the Law, they yet acquit you.

PONTALIER
But in Nouall, I doe condemne him thus.

CHARALOIS
I am slayne.

ROMONT
Can I looke on? Oh murderous wretch,
Thy challenge now I answere. So die with him.

CHARMI
A guard: disarme him.

ROMONT
I yeeld vp my sword
Vnforc'd. Oh Charaloys.

CHARALOIS
For shame, Romont,
Mourne not for him that dies as he hath liu'd,
Still constant and vnmou'd: what's falne vpon me,
Is by Heauens will, because I made my selfe
A Iudge in my owne cause without their warrant:

But he that lets me know thus much in death,
With all good men forgiue mee.

PONTALIER
I receiue
The vengeance, which my loue not built on vertue,
Has made me worthy, worthy of.

CHARMI
We are taught
By this sad president, how iust foeuer
Our reasons are to remedy our wrongs,
We are yet to leaue them to their will and power,
That to that purpose haue authority.
For you, Romont, although in your excuse
You may plead, what you did, was in reuenge
Of the dishonour done vnto the Court:
Yet since from vs you had not warrant for it,
We banish you the State: for these, they shall,
As they are found guilty or innocent,
Be set free, or suffer punishment.

[Exeunt **OMNES**.

FINIS

SOURCES

No source is known for the main plot of The Fatal Dowry. A Spanish original has been suspected, but it has never come to light. The stress laid throughout the action on that peculiarly Spanish conception of "the point of honor" (see under CRITICAL ESTIMATE, in consideration of the character of Charalois) is unquestionably suggestive of the land south of the Pyrenees, and we have an echo of Don Quixote in the exclamation of Charalois (III, i, 441): "Away, thou curious impertinent." The identification, however, of the situation at Aymer's house in IV, ii with a scene in Cervantes' El viejo celoso (Obras Completas De Cervantes, Tomo XII, p. 277) is extremely fanciful. The only similarity consists in the circumstance that in both, while the husband is on the stage, the wife, who, unknown to him, entertains a lover in the next room, is heard speaking within. But this is a spontaneous outcry on the part of Beaumelle, who does not suspect the proximity of her husband, and her discovery follows, and from this the denouement of the play; whereas in Cervantes' entremes the wife deliberately calls in bravado to her niece, who is also on-stage, and boasts of her lover,—and the husband thinks this is in jest, and nothing comes of it but comedy.

The theme of the son's redemption of his father's corpse by his own captivity is from the classical story of Cimon and Miltiades, as narrated by Valerius Maximus, De dictis factisque memorabilibus, etc. Lib. V, cap. III. De ingratis externorum: Bene egissent Athenienses cum Miltiade, si eum post trecenta millia

Persarum Marathone devicta, in exilium protinus misissent, ac non in carcere et vinculis mori coegissent; sed, ut puto, hactenus saevire adversus optime meritum abunde duxerunt: immo ne corpus quidem eius, sic expirare coacti sepulturae primus mandari passi sunt, quam filius eius Cimon eisdem vinculis se constrigendum traderet. Hanc hereditatem paternam maximi ducis filius, et futurus ipse aetatis suae dux maximus, solam se crevisse, catenas et carcerem, gloriari potuit.

In the version of Cornelius Nepos (Vitae, Cimon I) Cimon is incarcerated against his will.

The action of the play is given the historical setting of the later fifteenth century wars of Louis XI of France and Charles the Bold of Burgundy, although this background is extremely hazy. The hero's name is the title which Charles bore while heir-apparent to the Duchy of Burgundy; mention is made of Charles himself ("The warlike Charloyes," I, ii, 171), to Louis ("the subtill Fox of France, The politique Lewis," I, ii, 123-4), and to "the more desperate Swisse" (I, ii, 124), against whom Charles lost his life and the power of Burgundy was broken; while the three great defeats he suffered at their hands, Granson, Morat, Nancy, are named in I, ii, 170. Shortly after these disasters the events which the play sets forth must be supposed to occur; the parliament by which in our drama Dijon is governed was established by Louis XI when he annexed Burgundy in 1477 and thereby abolished her ducal independence.

COLLABORATION

It is doubtful if Massinger ever collaborated with any author whose manner harmonized as well with his own as did Field's. In his partnership with Decker in The Virgin Martyr, the alternate hands of the two dramatists afford a weird contrast. His union with Fletcher was less incongruous, but Fletcher was too much inclined to take the bit between his teeth to be a comfortable companion in double harness, and at all times his volatile, prodigal genius paired ill with the earnest, painstaking, not over-poetic moralist. But in Field Massinger found an associate whose connection with himself was not only congenial, but even beneficial, to the end that together they could achieve certain results of which either was individually incapable; just as it has been established was the case in the Middleton-Rowley collaboration. To a formal element of verse different, indeed, from Massinger's, but not obtrusively so, a certain moral fibre of his own (perhaps derived from his clerical antecedents), and a like familiarity with stage technique, Field added qualities which Massinger notably lacked, and thereby complemented him: a light and vigorous (if sometimes coarse) comic touch as opposed to Massinger's cumbrous humor; a freshness and first-hand acquaintance with life as opposed to Massinger's bookishness; a capacity to visualize and individualize character as opposed to Massinger's weakness for drawing types rather than people. The fruit of their joint endeavors testifies to a harmonious, conscientious, and mutually respecting partnership.

STAGE HISTORY—ADAPTATIONS—DERIVATIVES

Beyond the statement on the title-page of the 1632 Quarto, that The Fatal Dowry had been "often acted at the Private House in Blackfriars by his Majesties Servants," nothing is known of its early stage history. It was not revived after the Restoration, and until the publication of the Coxeter edition of Massinger seems to have been almost unknown. At last, in 1825, an emended version was placed upon the boards by no less an actor than the great Macready. January 5 of that year was the date, and Drury Lane the place, of its initial performance, Macready himself taking the part of Romont, Wallack—Charalois, Terry—Rochfort, and Mrs. W. West—Beaumelle. "The play was well acted and enthusiastically applauded," says Macready in his Reminiscences (p. 228); "its repetition for the following Tuesday was hailed most rapturously; but Friday came, and with it a crowded house, to find me laboring under such indisposition that it was with difficulty I could keep erect without support." Macready's serious illness cut short the run of the play, and when he was at length (April 11) able to take it up again, the interest of the public had abated, and it in consequence was repeated only a few times—seven being the total number of its performances.

The variant of The Fatal Dowry in which Macready acted was the work of Sheil, and involved substantial divergences. Romont's release from prison follows immediately upon Novall Senior's consent to his pardon, and in consequence, together with his conversation with Rochfort, is transferred from Act II to the close of Act I, while the redemption of Charalois takes place at the funeral of his father, which concludes Act II. For the scene between Beaumelle and her maids is substituted another coloquy of similar import but chastened tone. A brief scene of no especial significance is inserted at the beginning of Act III, in the interval between which and the preceding Act three weeks are supposed to have elapsed; the rest of Act III follows much the same course as the original, save that the application of Romont to Rochfort and his foiling by the stratagem of Beaumelle and Bellapert are omitted. A really notable departure is found in the discovery of the amour by Charalois. According to Sheil, Novall Junior and his mistress attempt to elope, but the note which appoints their rendezvous falls into Charalois' hands, and he waits for the lovers and surprises them, killing Novall off-stage. The Fifth Act opens with a scene of a few lines only, in which Beaumont bears to Rochfort a request from Charalois to meet him in the church yard. Then follows a lugubrious scene in the dead of night beside the tomb of the hero's father, to which place are transferred the reconciliation between Charalois and Romont, and the judgment of Rochfort! Beaumelle, however, does not appear during the trial, and upon the paternal sentence of doom, Charalois reveals her body, slain already by his hand. To the father he vindicates his action in much the same words as in Massinger's last court-room scene, and then, on the appearance of Novall Senior clamoring for vengeance and accompanied by the minions of the law, stabs himself.

The version of Sheil follows with but occasional exceptions the language of the original wherever possible. It makes some slight changes in the minor characters.

Sheil's redaction was also presented at Bath on February 18 and 21, Romont being acted by Hamblin, Charalois by Warde, Beaumelle by Miss E. Tree. "Hamblin never appeared to so much advantage—in the scene with Novall he reminded one strongly of John Kemble," says Genest (Hist. Dra. and Stage in Eng., IX, 322).

At Sadler's Wells, Samuel Phelps, who at that time was reviving a number of the old dramas, took the stage in The Fatal Dowry on August 27, 1845. This, however, was Sheil's version, and not the original play of Massinger and Field, as has been sometimes supposed. It ranked as one of his four chief productions of that year. He, too, chose for himself the part of Romont, which was considered by many his greatest quasi-tragic role. Marston appeared as Charalois, G. Bennett as Rochfort, and Miss Cooper as Beaumelle.

The Fatal Dowry in substantially its own proper form does not appear ever to have been acted after Jacobean times.

If the stage career of The Fatal Dowry has been meagre, not so the extent of its influence. Its literary parenthood begins before "the closing of the theatres" and continues even to our own day. As early as 1638 it was echoed in The Lady's Trial of Ford. Here the figures of Auria, Adurni, Aurelio, and Spinella correspond roughly with Charalois, young Novall, Romont, and Beaumelle respectively. Auria has gone to the wars, and in his absence his wife is pursued by Adurni, who sits at table with her in private, when Aurelio breaks in upon them, bursting open the doors. Spinella bitterly resents the intrusion and the aspersions of the intruder, and when, on the return home of Auria, Aurelio accuses her to him, it is without shaking his faith in her loyalty. Here the analogy ends: spite of Auria's incredulousness there is no rupture between the friends; Spinella establishes her innocence; and Adurni, while guilty enough in his intent against her, shows himself thereafter to be an essentially noble youth, who will defend to any length the lady's honor which has become subject to question through fault of his, and for this gallant reparation, is not only forgiven, but even cherished ever after by the husband he had sought to wrong.

The more steadily one regards the man John Ford and his work, the more probable does it appear that the relationship between The Fatal Dowry and The Lady's Trial is not one of mere reminiscence or influence, but of direct parentage. That strange and baleful figure, who seems almost a modern Decadent born out of his time, had a profound interest in moral problems, to the study of which he brought morbid ethical sensibilities scarce matched before the latter nineteenth century. (Witness his conception, in The Broken Heart, of a loveless marriage as tantamount to adultery.) Ford's talent for invention was deficient to the extent that he was hard put to it for plots. It is not at all unlikely that he surveyed the Massingerian tragedy, and, repelled by the conduct of its figures, exclaimed to himself: "I will write a play to centre around a situation as incriminating as that of Act III of The Fatal Dowry; but my personages will be worthier characters; I will show a lady who, spite of appearances, is of stainless innocence and vindicates her husband's trust in the face of evidence; I will show a friendship strong enough to endure an honestly mistaken aspersion put upon the chastity of a wife, though the charge is not for one moment credited; I will show that even the would-be seducer may be a fine fellow at bottom, and set forth a generous emulation in magnanimity between him and the husband. See how finely everything would work out with the right sort of people!" It is at least a plausible hypothesis.

Nicholas Rowe, who was the first modern editor of Shakespeare, contemplated also an edition of Massinger, but gave up the project that he might more safely plunder one of his plays. Rowe's famous tragedy, The Fair Penitent, was deliberately stolen from The Fatal Dowry. It appeared in 1703, and spite of a ludicrous accident which cut short its first run, took rank as one of the most celebrated dramas of the English stage. Rowe lived during the vogue of the "She-tragedy," while the canons of literary criticism of his day demanded a "regular," pseudo-classical form and a sententious tone. Accordingly, in his hands the chief figure in the play, as is evidenced by the change in title, becomes the guilty wife, here called Calista, who is "now the evil queen of the heroic plays; now the lachrymose moralizer;" the theme is indeed her story, not Altamont's (Charalois)—her seduction (prior to the nuptuals and before the opening of the play), her grief, her plight, her exposure, her death;—she holds the centre of the stage to the very end. The number of the dramatis personae is cut down to eight; all touches of comedy are excised; and the double plot of the original is unified by the bold stroke of throwing back to a time before the opening of the play the entire episode of the unburied corpse and the origin of the hero's friendship with the father of the heroine.

Discussions of the relative merits of The Fair Penitent and its source have been almost invariably acrimonious. Nor is this to be wondered at, for after reading the old tragedy with its severe dignity and noble restraint, one can scarce peruse without irritation the cloyingly melifluous, emasculated verse of Rowe—by turns grandiloquent and sentimental. The characterization of The Fair Penitent is, in the main, insipid, and while Rowe's heroine holds a commanding place in her drama to which Beaumelle does not pretend, the latter is a great deal more natural, and indeed, for that matter, far more truly a "penitent." An exception to the general insipidity is Lothario, who is the analogue of the insignificant Novall Junior—"the gay Lothario"—whose very name has been ever since a synonym for the graceful, graceless, devil-may-care libertine—whose figure has been the prototype of a long line of similar characters in English literature, beginning with Richardson's Lovelace and not yet closed with Anthony Hope's Rupert of Hentzau. Beside this striking creation, the seducer of Beaumelle shows poorly indeed; but it is doubtful if the old dramatists would have consented to paint such an attractive rogue, had they been able; they wanted their Novall to be just the cowardly, dandyfied thing they made him. Beyond the portrait of Lothario, small ground for praise can be found in The Fair Penitent. That part of the action of The Fatal Dowry which under Rowe's treatment antedates the rise of the curtain is narrated in the most stiffly mechanical sort of exposition; the action is developed by such threadbare theatrical devices as a lost letter and an overheard conversation; the voluble speeches of the several characters are, throughout, declamatory effusions almost unbelievably divorced from the apposite utterance of any rational human being under the circumstances. An Altamont who has been assured and reassured from his bride's own lips of her aversion for him can fling himself from a quarrel with his life-long friend in hysterical defence of her, to seek solace in her arms—

There if in any pause of love I rest
Breathless with bliss upon her panting breast,
In broken, melting accents I will swear,
Henceforth to trust my heart with none save her;

a Sciolto who has given his daughter a dagger with which to end her shame, and then has arrested her willing arm with the prayer that she will not dispatch herself until he is gone from the sight of her, can thereupon take leave of her with the statement:

There is I know not what of sad presage
That tells me I shall never see thee more.

The play, which enjoyed an immense fame, high contemporary appreciation, and a long career on the stage, remains a curious memorial of the taste of a bygone day.

It is noteworthy that in The Fair Penitent Horatio, as Romont in all modern reproductions of The Fatal Dowry, is the great acting part—not the husband.

In 1758 was produced at the Hay market a drama entitled The Insolvent or Filial Piety, from the pen of Aaron Hill. In the preface it is said—according to Genest (IV, 538)—"Wilks about 30 years before gave an old manuscript play, called the Guiltless Adulteress, to Theo. Cibber who was manager of what then was the Summer Company—after an interval of several years this play was judged to want a revisal to fit it for representation—Aaron Hill at the request of Theo. Cibber almost new wrote the whole, and the last act was entirely his in conduct, sentiment and diction." In reality, The Insolvent is The Fatal Dowry over again, altered to tragicomedy, and with the names of the characters changed. The first two Acts of Hill's play proceed much after the manner of its prototype, with close parallels in language. From thenceforward, however, the action diverges. The bride, Amelia, resists the further attentions of her former sweetheart. They are none the less observed and suspected by her husband's friend, who speaks of the matter to both her father and her lord. The former promises to observe her with watchful eye; Chalons, the husband, is at first resentful of the imputation, but presently yields to his friend's advice, that he pretend a two-days' journey, from which he will return unexpectedly. During his absence, his wife's maid introduces the lover into her mistress' chamber while Amelia sleeps. There Chalons surprises him kneeling beside the bed, and kills him. Amelia stabs herself, but the confession of her maid reveals her innocence, and her wound is pronounced not mortal.

It has been suggested (Biographia Dramatica, II, 228—quoted by Phelan, p. 59, and Schwarz, p. 74) that in Hill's Zara (adaptation of the Zaire of Voltaire), also, Nerestan's voluntary return to captivity in order to end that of his friends, whom he lacked the means to ransom with gold, was suggested by the behavior of Charalois; but this can be no more than a coincidence, as it here but reproduces what is in the French original.

A long interval, and finally, in the dawn of the twentieth century, there appeared the next and latest recrudescence of The Fatal Dowry. This was Der Graf von Charolais, ein Trauerspiel, by Richard Beer-Hofmann, disciple of the Neo-Romantic School or Vienna Decadents, a coterie built about the leadership of Hugo von Hofmannsthal. Beer-Hofmann's play—a five-Act tragedy in blank verse—was produced for the first time at the Neue Theatre, Berlin, on December 24, 1904, and was received with considerable acclaim. Unlike Rowe, he gives full credit to his source, from which he has drawn no less extensively than the author of The Fair Penitent. Unlike Rowe, he goes back to the old dramatists in the matter of construction, placing upon the stage once more the episode of the unburied corpse and the noble son; he even outdoes The Fatal Dowry in this respect, by allowing the first half of his plot three Acts instead of two, with only two Acts for the amour and its tragic consequences. In his hands the hero again becomes the central figure; in fact, the three principal versions of this donnee suggest by their titles their respective viewpoints: The Fatal Dowry; The Fair Penitent; Der Graf von Charolais. DER GRAF VON CHAROLAIS, be it observed;—this new redaction is no longer the tale of a "fatal dowry;" no longer is the first part of the dual theme merely introductory and accessory—it is coördinate with the second. Beer-Hofmann has sought to achieve a kind of unity from his double plot by making his fundamental theme not the adulterous intrigue, but the destiny of Charolais, thus converting the play into a Tragedy of Fate, which pursues the hero inexorably through all his life. This strictly classical motif animating the donnee of a Jacobean play reproduced in the twentieth century presents, as might be expected, the aspect of an exotic growth, which is not lessened by the extreme sensuousness of treatment throughout, such as has always been one of the cardinal and distinctive qualities of the Decadent School the world over. But as a contrast in the dramatic technique and verse of Jacobean and modern times, Der Graf von Charolais is extremely interesting. The difference is striking between the severe simplicity of three centuries ago, and the elaborate stagecraft of to-day, its insistence on detail, and studied care in the portraiture of minor characters. Yet minutia do not make tragedy, and while their superficial realism and the congeniality of the contemporary point of view undeniably lend to Beer-Hofmann's redaction a palatability and a power to interest and appeal which its original does not possess to the modern reader, yet a discriminating critic will turn back to the old play with a feeling that, for all its stiffness and conventions, he breathes there a more vital air. To the enrichment of his theme Beer-Hofmann contributes every ingenious effect possible to symbolism, delicate suggestion, and scenic device; this exterior decoration is gorgeous in its color and seductive warmth, but no amount of such stuff can compensate for the fundamental flaw in the crucial episode of his tragedy. In spite of the care which he has lavished on the scene between his heroine and her seducer, the surrender of the wife—three years married, a mother, and loving both husband and child—remains insufficiently motivated and sheerly inexplicable, and by this vital, inherent defect the play must fall. Moreover, it lacks a hero. Romont can no longer play the main part he did in former versions; he is reduced to a mere shadow. In a tragedy of Fate, which blights a man's career, phase by phase, with persistent, relentless hand, that man must necessarily be the central figure, and, of right, should be an imposing figure—a protagonist at once gigantic and appealing, who will draw all hearts to him in pity and terror at the helpless, hopeless struggle of over-matched greatness and worth; whereas Charolais—

The case of Charolais is peculiar. A priori we should expect him to be just such a personage, yet his conduct throughout is best explainable as that of a man dominated, not by noble impulses, but by an extreme egoism—a man acutely responsive alike to his sense-impressions and his feverish imagination, and possessed of an exaggerated squeamishness towards the ugly and the unpleasant. When, in the First Act, he bursts into tears, he confesses it is not for his father that he weeps, but for his own hard lot; he suffers from his repugnance to the idea of his father's corpse rotting above ground—a repugnance so intolerable to him that he will yield his liberty to escape it. He purposes to cashier the innkeeper because the sight of the lecherous patrons of his hostelry has disgusted him, and he alters his resolve and forgives the fellow, not from any considerations of mercy, but because the mental picture of the man's distress tortures him. And by similar personal repugnances reacting on egoism is his behavior in the denouement to be accounted for, and in this light becomes logically credible and clearly understood. Few practices are more hazardous or unjust than judging an artist by his objective creations; but an ignoble protagonist, as Charolais is represented, is in such ill accord with any conceivable purpose on the part of Beer-Hofmann, and so unlikely to have been intended by him, that one cannot help strongly suspecting that the author unconsciously projected himself into the character and thus revealed his own nature and point of view. In any case he has presented for his hero a whimperer who can command neither our sympathy nor our respect when he cries above the bodies of his benefactor and her who is that benefactor's daughter, his own wife, and the mother of his child:

Ist dies Stück denn aus,
Weil jene starb? Und ich? An mich denkt keiner?

We have come a long way from Massinger and Field and the early seventeenth century. The shadow of the old dramatists reaches far, even to our own time; we have seen their play redeveloped, but never improved upon, by pseudo-classicist, and popularizer, and Decadent hyper-aesthete. That which was the vulnerable point in the original production—its two-fold plot—has been still for every imitator a stone of stumbling. Rowe tried to escape it by the suppression of the antecedent half, and the fraction which remained in his hand was an artificial thing without the breath of life, that had to be attenuated and padded out with speechifying to fill the compass of its five Acts. Beer-Hofmann tried to escape it by superimposing an idea not proper to the story, and beneath the weight of this his tragedy collapsed in the middle, for its addition over-packed the drama, and left him not room enough to make convincing the conduct of his characters. The first essayers, who attacked in straightforward fashion their unwieldy theme, succeeded best; all attempts to obviate its essential defect have marred rather than mended. Perhaps the theme is by its nature unsuited to dramatic treatment, and yet there is much that is dramatic about that theme, as is evinced by the fact that playwrights have been unable to let it lie.

PHILIP MASSINGER – A SHORT BIOGRAPHY

Very few materials exist for a life of Massinger beyond the entries of the Parish Register or the College Books, and a few slender intimations scattered here and there in the dedications to his plays. From these scanty sources the following brief memoir is derived.

Our author was born at Salisbury[1] in the year 1584: he was the son of Arthur Massinger, a gentleman in the service of Henry, the second Earl of Pembroke[2]. We must not suppose, from his being thus attached to the family of a nobleman, that the father of our poet was a person of inferior birth and station. In those days the word servant carried with it no sense of degradation. The great lords and officers of the court numbered inferior nobles among their followers. We read, in Cavendish's Life of Wolsey, that "my Lord Percy, the son and heir of the Earl of Northumberland, attended upon and was servitor to the lord-cardinal[3]:" and from the situation which Arthur Massinger held in the household of so high and influential a person as the Earl of Pembroke, we might be justly led to argue rather favourably than unfavourably of his family and his connexions. "There were," says Mr. Gifford, "many considerations which united to render this state of dependance respectable and even honourable. The secretaries, clerks, and assistants, of various departments, were not then, as now, nominated by the government, but left to the choice of the person who held the employment; and as no particular dwelling was officially set apart for their residence, they were entertained in the house of their principal. That communication, too, between noblemen of power and trust, both of a public and private nature, which is now committed to the post, was in those days managed by confidential servants, who were despatched from one to the other, and even to the sovereign[4];" and, indeed, the father of our poet himself was, we know, in one instance thus employed as the bearer of communications from his patron to Elizabeth. We read in The Sidney Letters[5], "Mr. Massinger is newly come up from the Earl of Pembroke with letters to the queen for his lordship's leave to be away this St. George's Day." This was an errand which would not have been intrusted to the execution of any inconsiderable person: unimportant as the occasion may appear to us, it would not have been regarded in that light by Elizabeth; for no monarch ever exacted from the nobility, and particularly from her officers of state, a more rigid and scrupulous compliance with stated order than this princess.

With regard to the early youth of Massinger, we possess no information whatever. Mr. Gifford supposes that it might have been passed at Wilton, a seat belonging to the Earl of Pembroke, in the neighbourhood of Salisbury; but this mode of disposing of his early years rests on a very improbable conjecture. It may occasionally have happened that the child of a favourite dependant was admitted as the companion of the younger branches of the patron's family, and allowed to receive his education among them; but this was certainly not an ordinary case; and, like Cavendish, a large majority of the great man's servants and dependants "left wife and children, home and family, rest and quietness, only to serve him[6]."—Massinger was most likely educated at the grammar-school of Salisbury, where many distinguished characters have received the rudiments of their education, among whom the elegant and accomplished Addison is to be numbered. But wherever the first years of our poet's life may have been spent, and whatever may have been the nature of his education, we know that at the age of eighteen (May 14, 1602) he was entered at the university of Oxford, and became a commoner of St. Alban's Hall[7].

Massinger resided at Oxford about four years, and then abruptly left it, without taking any degree. The cause of this sudden departure is ascribed by Mr. Gifford to the death of his father, from whom his supplies were derived: but Davies relates a very different story, and asserts that the Earl of Pembroke, who had sent him to the university and maintained him there, withdrew the necessary allowance in consequence of his having misapplied the time demanded for severer studies, in the pursuit of a more attractive but less profitable description of literature. Each opinion is equally ungrounded on the basis of any substantial evidence, and rests almost entirely on the imagination of the biographer: what slight authority there is favours the latter supposition, which, perhaps, on the whole, is most consistent with the known circumstances of the case. Anthony Wood, who was born, lived, and died at Oxford; who spent his time in collecting and recording the gossip which circulated in the university respecting the characters and conduct of its more distinguished sons; and whose evidence, however indifferent it may be, is the best that can be obtained upon the subject, confirms the representation of Davies:—"Massinger," says Wood, "gave his mind more to poetry and romance, for about four years or more, than to logic and philosophy, which he ought to have done, as he was patronised to that end." This passage corroborates the account of Davies so far as to intimate that patronage was afforded to our author, and that cause of dissatisfaction was given to the patron; but it goes no farther: it does not even state to whom the poet was indebted for assistance, nor that the misapplication of his academic hours was at all resented by the friend from whom the assistance was received: but still Wood is very probably correct in his information that other than his paternal funds were depended upon for maintaining Massinger at the university; and if such was the case, there can be no question from whose hands they must have proceeded; while the simple fact of his having been totally neglected, from the time of his father's death, by the whole of the Pembroke family, till after the demise of the earl, carries with it a strong suspicion that some offence was committed on the side of the poet, and tenaciously remembered on the side of the peer. Henry, the second Earl of Pembroke, died (1601) the year before Massinger was admitted at Oxford; and William, the third earl, to whom the father of Massinger continued attached during life, is universally and justly considered one of the brightest ornaments of the courts of Elizabeth and James. He was a man of generous and liberal disposition; the distinguished patron of arts and learning; and a lover of poetry, which he himself cultivated with some degree of success. It is not probable—it is impossible—that such a man should have allowed the highly talented son of an old and faithful servant of his family to be checked in his course of study, and abandoned to maintain, through the early years of life, a single-handed contest with adversity, for the want of that pecuniary aid which he could have yielded and never missed, unless some strong and decided cause of displeasure had existed. Had Massinger been merely forced to leave the university, as Mr. Gifford supposes, because the funds necessary to maintain him there had failed with the life of his father, we impute an act of illiberality to the Earl of Pembroke which is inconsistent with the whole tenor of his life and character. From whatever source the expenses of our author's education were originally defrayed, their suddenly ceasing argues in favour of the account intimated by Wood and detailed by Davies. If his father had, during his life, supported him at the university, there must have been some reason for the earl's not continuing that support when the father of Massinger was no more; and perhaps the most honourable supposition for both parties is that which represents the earl as offended by the bent of our author's studies and pursuits. By adopting this view of the case we are saved from the painful necessity of either assuming, on the one hand, that a nobleman distinguished among the most amiable characters of his age allowed a highly gifted and meritorious young man, a natural dependant of his house, to languish in the want of that countenance and protection on which he had an hereditary claim; or, on the other hand, that Massinger had incurred the displeasure of his natural and hereditary patron by the commission of some more crying offence.

Every, even the slightest, surmise of Mr. Gifford is deserving attention and respect; but I cannot admit the supposition by which he would account for the alienation that subsisted between the Earl of Pembroke and our author. That distinguished critic has inferred, from the religious sentiments contained in The Virgin Martyr, that Massinger was a Roman catholic, and for that cause neglected by the protector of his father. But if the intimations scattered through this play and others should be received as sufficient evidence of the faith of Massinger, we must, on similar evidence—the intimations contained in Measure for Measure, for instance—conclude that the religion of Shakspeare was the same; and then we are cast back upon our old difficulty, and have to explain why William Earl of Pembroke, a celebrated patron of literary men, and of dramatists in particular, scorned to yield his notice to the catholic Massinger, while (to use the expression of Heminge and Condell) he "prosequuted" the catholic Shakspeare and "his works with so much favour[8]?" There are many reasons for believing Shakspeare to have been a member of the church of Rome; and the patronage afforded him by the Earl of Pembroke proves, that that nobleman extended his liberality to men of genius without any regard to distinctions of faith; but, on the other hand, we have no just grounds for assuming that Massinger really did hold the same opinions. The only evidence we have upon this point, that afforded by the general tone of his writings, is of a most vague and superficial description. What, in fact, can be inferred from it? We may from such a source derive very satisfactory information respecting the sentiments which would be favourably received by the audience, but very little respecting those of the author. The truth is, that though the national religion was reformed in its liturgy and articles, the feelings, prejudices, and superstitions of the people were still almost entirely catholic; and Massinger, like any other dramatic author, writing for the amusement of the people, necessarily addressed them in a language they would understand, and with sentiments that accorded with their own. Besides, as a poet, he would never carry his theological distinctions to his literary labours: Voltaire himself is catholic in his tragedies; and Massinger naturally adopted the creed which was most suitable to the purposes of poetry, and afforded the most picturesque ceremonies and romantic situations. I feel inclined, therefore, to dismiss entirely the theory suggested by Mr. Gifford, for these two reasons; first, supposing our author to have been a catholic, we have no reason for condemning the Earl of Pembroke as a bigot and a persecutor, who would close his eyes to the merits of so great an author, because his faith did not tally with his own; and, secondly, we have no sufficient grounds for supposing him to have been a catholic at all. But with regard to all such visionary conjectures, thinking is literally a waste of thought.

Whatever may have been the nature of Massinger's studies at Oxford, it is quite certain, from the general character of his works, that his time could not have been wasted there; and his literary acquirements, at the period of his leaving the university, appear to have been multifarious and extensive. He was about two-and-twenty (1606) when he arrived in London, where, as he more than once observes, he was driven by his necessities, and somewhat inclined, perhaps, by the peculiar bent of his talents, to dedicate himself to the service of the stage.

The theatre, when Massinger first took up his abode in the metropolis, must have presented attractions of all others the most calculated to excite the interest, and inspire the imagination, of a young man of sensibility, taste, and education like our poet. No art ever attained a more rapid maturity than the dramatic art in England. The people had, indeed, been long accustomed to a species of exhibition, called MIRACLES or MYSTERIES, founded on sacred subjects, and performed by the ministers of religion themselves, on the holy festivals, in or near the churches, and designed to instruct the ignorant in the leading facts of sacred history[9]. From the occasional introduction of allegorical characters, such as Faith, Death, Hope, or Sin, into these religious dramas, representations of another kind, called MORALITIES, had by degrees arisen, of which the plots were more artificial, regular, and connected, and which were entirely formed of such personifications: but the first rough draught of a regular tragedy and comedy—Lord Sackville's Gorboduc, and Still's Gammer Gurton's Needle[10]—were not produced till within the latter half of the sixteenth century, and little more than twenty years before the stage acquired its highest splendour in the productions of Shakspeare.

About the end of the sixteenth century, the attention of the public began to be more generally directed to the drama; and it throve most admirably beneath the cheering beams of popular favour. The theatrical performances which in the early part of Elizabeth's reign had been exhibited on temporary stages, erected in such halls or apartments as the actors could procure, or, more generally, in the yards of the larger inns, while the spectators surveyed them from the surrounding windows and galleries, began to find more convenient and permanent habitations. About the year 1569, a regular playhouse, under the appropriate name of The Theatre, was erected. It is supposed to have stood somewhere in Blackfriars; and, three years after the commencement of this establishment, the queen, yielding to her own inclination for such amusements, and disregarding the remonstrances of the Puritans, granted licence and authority to the servants of the Earl of Leicester ("for the recreation of her loving subjects, as for her own solace and pleasure when she should think good to see them") to exercise their occupation throughout the whole realm of England. From this time the number of theatres increased with the increasing demands of the people. Various noblemen had their respective companies of performers, who were associated as their servants, and acted under their protection; and when Massinger left Oxford, and commenced dramatic author, there were no less than seven principal theatres open in the metropolis.

With respect to the interior arrangements, there were very few points of difference between our modern theatres and those of the days of Massinger. The prices of admission, indeed, were considerably cheaper: to the boxes the entrance was a shilling; to the pit and galleries only sixpence. Sixpence also was the price paid for stools upon the stage; and these seats, as we learn from Decker's Gull's Hornbook, were particularly affected by the wits and critics of the time. The conduct of the audience was less restrained by the sense of public decorum, and smoking tobacco, playing at cards, eating and drinking, were generally prevalent among them. The hours of performance were also earlier: the play commencing at one o'clock. During the representation a flag was unfurled at the top of the theatre; and the stage, according to the universal practice of the age, was strewn with rushes; but, in all other respects, the theatres of Elizabeth and James's days seem to have borne a perfect resemblance to our own. They had their pit, where the inferior class of spectators, the groundlings, vented their clamorous censure or approbation; they had their boxes—rooms as they were called—to which the right of exclusive admission was engaged by the night, for the more affluent portion of the audience; and there were again the galleries, or scaffoldings above the boxes, for those who were content to purchase less commodious situations at a cheaper rate. On the stage, in the same manner, the appointments appear to have been nearly of the same description as at present. The curtain divided the audience from the actors, which, at the third sounding, not indeed of the bell, but of the trumpet, was drawn for the commencement of the performance. Malone, in his account of the ancient theatre, supposes that there were no moveable scenes; that a permanent elevation of about nine feet was raised at the back of the stage, from which, in many of the old plays, part of the dialogue was spoken; and that there was a private box on each side this platform. Such an arrangement would have destroyed all theatrical illusion; and it seems extraordinary that any spectators should desire to fix themselves in a station where they could have seen nothing but the backs and trains of the performers; but, as Malone himself acknowledges the spot to have been inconvenient, and that "it is not very easy to ascertain the precise situation where these boxes really were[11]", it may very reasonably be presumed, that they were not placed in the position that the historian of the English stage has supposed. As to the permanent floor, or upper stage, of which he speaks, he may or may not be correct in his statement. All that his quotations upon the subject really establish is, that in the old, as in the modern theatre, when the actor was to speak from a window, or balcony, or the walls of a fortress, the requisite ingenuity was not wanting to contrive a representation of the place. But with regard to the use of painted moveable scenery, it is not possible, from the very circumstances of the case, to believe him correct in his theory. Such a contrivance could not have escaped our ancestors. All the materials were ready to their hands. They had not to invent for themselves, but merely to adapt an old invention to that peculiar purpose; and at a time when every better-furnished apartment was adorned with tapestry; when even the rooms of the commonest taverns were hung with painted cloths; while all the materials were constantly before their eyes, we can hardly believe our forefathers to have been so deficient in ingenuity, as to have missed the simple contrivance of converting the common ornaments of their walls into the decorations of their theatres. But, in fact, the use of scenery was almost co-existent with the introduction of dramatic representations in this country. In the Chester Mysteries (1268), the most ancient and complete collection of the kind which we possess, is found the following stage direction: "Then Noe shall go into the arke with all his familye, his wife excepte. The arke must be boarded round about; and upon the boardes all the beastes and fowles, hereafter rehearsed, must be painted, that their wordes may agree with their pictures[12]." In this passage we have a clear reference to a painted scene. It is not likely that, in the lapse of three centuries, while all other arts were in a state of rapid improvement, and the art of dramatic writing, perhaps, more rapidly and successfully improved than any other, the art of theatrical decoration should have alone stood still. It is not improbable that their scenes were few; and that they were varied, as occasion might require, by the introduction of different pieces of stage furniture. Mr. Gifford, who adheres to the opinions of Malone, says, "A table with a pen and ink thrust in, signified that the stage was a counting-house; if these were withdrawn and two stools put in their place, it was then a tavern[13]." And this might be perfectly satisfactory as long as the business of the play was supposed to be passing within doors; but when it was removed to the open air, such meagre devices would no longer be sufficient to guide the imagination of the audience, and some new method must have been adopted to indicate the place of action. After giving the subject very considerable attention, I cannot help thinking that Steevens was right in rejecting Malone's theory, and concluding that the spectators were, as at the present day, assisted in following the progress of the story by means of painted moveable scenery. This opinion is confirmed by the ancient stage directions. In the folio Shakspeare, 1623, we read "Enter Brutus in his orchard; Enter Timon in the woods; Enter Timon from the cave." In Coriolanus, "Marcius follows them to the gates and is shut in." Innumerable instances of the same kind might be cited to prove that the ancient stage was not so defective in the necessary decorations as some antiquaries of great authority would represent. "It may be added," says Steevens, "that the dialogue of our old dramatists has such perpetual reference to objects supposed visible to the audience, that the want of scenery could not have failed to render many of the descriptions absurd. Banquo examines the outside of Inverness castle with such minuteness, that he distinguishes even the nests which the martens had built under the projecting part of its roof. Romeo, standing in a garden, points to the tops of fruit-trees gilded by the moon. The prologue speaker to the second part of Henry the Fourth expressly shows the spectators 'This worm-eaten hold of ragged stone,' in which Northumberland was lodged. Iachimo takes the most exact inventory of every article in Imogen's bed-chamber, from the silk and silver of which her tapestry was wrought, down to the Cupids that support her andirons. Had not the inside of the apartment, with its proper furniture, been represented, how ridiculous must the action of Iachimo have appeared! He must have stood looking out of the room for the particulars supposed to be visible within it." The works of Massinger would afford innumerable instances of a similar kind to vindicate the opinion which Steevens has asserted on the testimony of Shakspeare alone. But on this subject there is one passage which appears to me quite conclusive. Must not all the humour of the mock play in The Midsummer Night's Dream have been entirely lost, unless the audience before whom it was performed were accustomed to all the embellishments requisite to give effect to a dramatic representation, and could consequently estimate the absurdity of those shallow contrivances and mean substitutes for scenery devised by the ignorance of the clowns[14]?

In only one respect do I perceive any material difference between the mode of representation at the time of Massinger and at present: in his day, the female parts were performed by boys. This custom, which must in many cases have materially injured the illusion of the scene, was in others of considerable advantage: it furnished the stage with a succession of youths, regularly educated for the art, to fill, in every department of the drama, the characters suited to their age. When the lad had become too tall for Juliet, he had acquired the skill, and was most admirably fitted, both in age and appearance, for performing the part which Garrick considered the most difficult on the stage, because it needed "an old head upon young shoulders," the ardent and arduous character of Romeo. When the voice had "the mannish crack," that rendered the youth unfit to appear as the representative of the gentle Imogen, the stage possessed in him the very person that was wanting to do justice to the princely sentiments of Arviragus or Guiderius[15].

Such was the state of the stage when Massinger arrived in the metropolis, and dedicated his talents to its service. He joined a splendid fraternity, for Shakspeare, Jonson, Beaumont, Fletcher, Shirley, were then flourishing at the height of their reputation, and the full vigour of their genius. Massinger came among them no unworthy competitor for such honours and emoluments as the theatre could afford. Of the honours, indeed, he seems to have reaped a very fair and equitable portion; of the emoluments, the harvest was less abundant. In those days, very little pecuniary reward was to be gained by the dramatic poet, unless, as indeed was most frequently the case, he added the profession of the actor to that of the author, and recited the verses which he wrote. The distinguished performers of that time, Alleyn, Burbage, Heminge, Condell, Shakspeare, all appear to have died in independent, if not affluent, circumstances; but the remuneration obtained by the poet was most miserably curtailed. The price given at the theatre for a new play fluctuated between ten and twenty pounds; the copyright, if the piece was printed, might produce from six to ten pounds more; in addition to these sums, the dedication-fee may be reckoned, the usual amount of which was forty shillings. Our author appears to have produced about two or three plays every year. Most of them were successful; but, even with this industry and good fortune, his annual income would rarely have exceeded fifty pounds: and we cannot, therefore, feel surprised at finding him continually speaking of his necessities; or that the only existing document connected with his life should be one that represents him in a state of pecuniary embarrassment.

Among the papers of Dulwich College, the indefatigable Mr. Malone discovered the following letter tripartite, which, coming from persons of such deserved celebrity, cannot fail of interesting the reader.

"To our most loving friend, Mr. Phillip Hinchlow, esquire, these.

"Mr. Hinchlow,

"You understand our unfortunate extremitie, and I doe not thincke you so void of Christianitie but that you would throw so much money into the Thames as wee request now of you, rather than endanger so many innocent lives. You know there is xl. more, at least, to be receaved of you for the play. We desire you to lend us vl. of that, which shall be allowed to you; without which, we cannot be bayled, nor I play any more till this be dispatch'd. It will lose you xxl. ere the end of the next weeke, besides the hindrance of the next new play. Pray, sir, consider our cases with humanity, and now give us cause to acknowledge you our true freind in time of neede. Wee have entreated Mr. Davison to deliver this note, as well to witness your love as our promises, and alwayes acknowledgement to be ever

"Your most thankfull and loving friends,
"NAT. FIELD[16]."

"The money shall be abated out of the money remayns for the play of Mr. Fletcher and ours.
"ROB. DABORNE[17]."

"I have ever found you a true loving friend to mee, and in soe small a suite, it beinge honest, I hope you will not fail us.

"PHILIP MASSINGER."

Indorsed.
"Received by mee, Robert Davison, of Mr. Hinchlow, for the use of Mr. Daboerne, Mr. Feeld, Mr. Messenger, the sum of vl.
"ROB. DAVISON[18]."

The occasion of the distress in which these three distinguished persons were involved it is not possible to fathom. We may imagine a thousand emergencies, either creditable or discreditable to the fame of the writers, with which the letter would perfectly tally; but, on such slight and vague intimations, no ingenuity could determine which was most likely to be correct. But from the document a circumstance is ascertained, which, before its discovery, had been called in question. Sir Aston Cockayne, a friend of Massinger, had asserted in a volume of poems, published in 1658, that our author had written in conjunction with Fletcher; Davies doubted this report, but the above letter establishes the fact beyond the possibility of dispute.

Massinger is known to have produced thirty-seven plays for the stage, a list of which is given at the conclusion of this memoir. Sixteen entire plays and the fragment of another, The Parliament of Love, alone are extant. No less than eleven of his productions, in manuscript, were in possession of Mr. Warburton (Somerset Herald), and destroyed with the rest of that gentleman's invaluable collection by his cook, who, ignorant of their worth, used them as waste paper for the purposes of the kitchen.

The great and various merits of the works of Massinger will be better seen in the following volumes than in any elaborate, critical dissertation. If our author be compared with the other dramatic writers of his age, we cannot long hesitate where to place him. More natural in his characters and more poetical in his diction than Jonson or Cartwright, more elevated and nervous than Fletcher, the only writers who can be supposed to contest his pre-eminence, Massinger ranks immediately under Shakspeare himself. Our poet excels, perhaps, more in the description than in the expression of passion; this may in some measure be ascribed to his attention to the fable: while his scenes are managed with consummate skill, the lighter shades of character and sentiment are lost in the tendency of each part to the catastrophe. The melody, force, and variety of his versification are always remarkable. The prevailing beauties of his productions are dignity and elegance; their predominant fault is want of passion.

Massinger's last play—which is unfortunately lost—The Anchoress of Pausilippo, was acted Jan. 26, 1640, about six weeks before his death, which happened on the 17th of March, 1640. He went to bed in good health, says Langbaine, and was found dead in the morning, in his own house on the Bankside. He was buried in the churchyard of St. Saviour's, and the comedians paid the last sad duty to his name, by attending him to the grave.

It does not appear, though every stone and every fragment of a stone has been carefully examined, that any monument or inscription of any kind marked the place where his dust was deposited. "The memorial of his mortality," says Gifford, "is given with a pathetic brevity, which accords but too well with the obscure and humble passages of his life: March 20, 1639-40, buried Philip Massinger, A STRANGER."

Such is all the information that remains to us of this distinguished poet. But though we are ignorant of every circumstance respecting him but that he lived, wrote, and died, we may yet form some idea of his personal character from the recommendatory poems prefixed to his several plays, in which, as Mr.

Gifford justly observes, the language of his panegyrists, though warm, expresses an attachment apparently derived not so much from his talents as his virtues: he is their beloved, much-esteemed, dear, worthy, deserving, honoured, long-known, and long-loved friend. All the writers of his life represent him as a man of singular modesty, gentleness, candour, and affability; nor does it appear that he ever made or found an enemy.

FOOTNOTES

[1] The register of his birth is not to be found, but all writers of his life agree in naming this city as the place of his nativity; and their account is corroborated by the college entry, which styles him Salisburiensis.

[2] Dedication to The Bondman.

[3] Singer's edition, p. 120.

[4] Introduction to the Works of Massinger, p. xxxviii.

[5] Vol. ii. p. 933.

[6] Life of Wolsey, p. 517.

[7] The entry in the college book styles him "Phillip Massinger, Salisburiensis, generosi filius."

[8] Dedication to the folio edition of Shakspeare.

[9] Indulgences were granted to those who attended the representation of them.

[10] Gorboduc appeared in 1562; Gammer Gurton, in 1566.

[11] Reed's Shakspeare, vol. iii. p. 83, note 3.

[12] Reed's Shakspeare, vol. iii. p. 15.

[13] Gifford's Massinger, vol. i. p. 103.

[14] This question ought to be set at rest, methinks, by the following extract from the Book of Revels, the oldest that exists, in the office of the auditors of the imprest: "Mrs. Dane, the lynnen dealer, for canvass to paynte for houses for the players, and other properties, as monsters, great hollow trees, and such other, twenty dozen ells, 12l."—See Boswell's Shakspeare, vol. iii. p. 364, et seq.

[15] The first woman who appeared in a regular drama, on a public stage, played Desdemona, about the year 1660. Her name is unknown.

[16] Nat. Field. This celebrated actor played female parts. He was the author of two comedies: A Woman's a Weathercock, 1612, and Amends for Ladies, 1618. He also assisted Massinger in The Fatal Dowry.

[17] Robert Daborne was the author of two plays: The Christian turned Turk, 1612, and The poor Man's Comfort, 1655. He was a gentleman of liberal education, master of arts, and in holy orders. It is supposed that he had preferment in Ireland. A sermon by him, preached at Waterford, in 1618, is extant.

[18] Additions to Malone's Hist. Account of Eng. Stage, p. 488.

PHILIP MASSINGER – A CONCISE BIBLIOGRAPHY

As would be expected many works from this time not longer exist either in part or their entirety. Further many playwrights collaborated on plays or revised them for later performances and we have used the latest position known on each of them for the bibliography below..

Solo Plays

The Maid of Honour, tragicomedy (c. 1621; printed 1632)
The Duke of Milan, tragedy (c. 1621–3; printed 1623, 1638)
The Unnatural Combat, tragedy (c. 1621–6; printed 1639)
The Bondman, tragicomedy (licensed 3 December 1623; printed 1624)
The Renegado, tragicomedy (licensed 17 April 1624; printed 1630)
The Parliament of Love, comedy (licensed 3 November 1624; MS)
A New Way to Pay Old Debts, comedy (c. 1625; printed 1632)
The Roman Actor, tragedy (licensed 11 October 1626; printed 1629)
The Great Duke of Florence, tragicomedy (licensed 5 July 1627; printed 1636)
The Picture, tragicomedy (licensed 8 June 1629; printed 1630)
The Emperor of the East, tragicomedy (licensed 11 March 1631; printed 1632)
Believe as You List, tragedy (rejected by the censor in January, but licensed 6 May 1631; MS)
The City Madam, comedy (licensed 25 May 1632; printed 1658)
The Guardian, comedy (licensed 31 October 1633; printed 1655)
The Bashful Lover, tragicomedy (licensed 9 May 1636; printed 1655)

Collaborations with John Fletcher

Sir John van Olden Barnavelt, tragedy (August 1619; MS)
The Little French Lawyer, comedy (c. 1619–23; printed 1647)
A Very Woman, tragicomedy (c. 1619–22; licensed 6 June 1634; printed 1655)
The Custom of the Country, comedy (c. 1619–23; printed 1647)
The Double Marriage, tragedy (c. 1619–23; Printed 1647)
The False One, history (c. 1619–23; printed 1647)
The Prophetess, tragicomedy (licensed 14 May 1622; printed 1647)
The Sea Voyage, comedy (licensed 22 June 1622; printed 1647)
The Spanish Curate, comedy (licensed 24 October 1622; printed 1647)
The Lovers' Progress or The Wandering Lovers, tragicomedy (licensed 6 Dec 1623; rev 1634; printed 1647)
The Elder Brother, comedy (c. 1625; printed 1637).

Collaborations with John Fletcher and Francis Beaumont

Thierry and Theodoret, tragedy (c. 1607?; printed 1621)

The Coxcomb, comedy (1608–10; printed 1647)
Beggars' Bush, comedy (c. 1612–15?; revised 1622?; printed 1647)
Love's Cure, comedy (c. 1612–15?; revised 1625?; printed 1647).

Collaborations with John Fletcher and Nathan Field

The Honest Man's Fortune, tragicomedy (1613; printed 1647)
The Queen of Corinth, tragicomedy (c. 1616–18; printed 1647)
The Knight of Malta, tragicomedy (c. 1619; printed 1647).

Collaborations with Nathan Field

The Fatal Dowry, tragedy (c. 1619, printed 1632); adapted by Nicholas Rowe: The Fair Penitent

Collaborations with John Fletcher, John Ford, and William Rowley, or John Webster

The Fair Maid of the Inn, comedy (licensed 22 January 1626; printed 1647).

Collaborations with John Fletcher, Ben Jonson, and George Chapman

Rollo Duke of Normandy, or The Bloody Brother, tragedy (c. 1616–24; printed 1639).

Collaborations with Thomas Dekker:

The Virgin Martyr, tragedy (licensed 6 October 1620; printed 1622).

Collaborations with Thomas Middleton and William Rowley:

The Old Law, comedy (c. 1615–18; printed 1656).

www.ingramcontent.com/pod-product-compliance
Lightning Source LLC
LaVergne TN
LVHW020644100826
845148LV00012B/2329

9781787372979